God-Talk

OTHER BOOKS BY DAVID NOVAK

Law and Theology in Judaism I
Suicide and Morality
Law and Theology in Judaism II
The Image of the Non-Jew in Judaism, 1st edition
Halakhah in a Theological Dimension
Jewish-Christian Dialogue: A Jewish Justification
Jewish Social Ethics
The Theology of Nahmanides—Systematically Presented
The Election of Israel: The Idea of the Chosen People
Natural Law in Judaism
Covenantal Rights: A Study in Jewish Political Theory
The Jewish Social Contract: An Essay in Political Theology
Talking with Christians: Musings of a Jewish Theologian
The Sanctity of Human Life
In Defense of Religious Liberty
Tradition in the Public Square: A David Novak Reader
The Image of the Non-Jew in Judaism, 2nd revised edition
Natural Law: A Jewish, Christian, and Islamic Trialogue
(with Anver Emon and Matthew Levering)
Zionism and Judaism: A New Theory
Jewish Justice: The Contested Limits of Nature, Law, and Covenant
Athens and Jerusalem: God, Humans, and Nature

God-Talk

The Heart of Judaism

David Novak

ROWMAN & LITTLEFIELD
Lanham • Boulder • New York • London

Published by Rowman & Littlefield
An imprint of The Rowman & Littlefield Publishing Group, Inc.
4501 Forbes Boulevard, Suite 200, Lanham, Maryland 20706
www.rowman.com

86-90 Paul Street, London EC2A 4NE

British Library Cataloguing in Publication Information Available

Library of Congress Cataloging-in-Publication Data

Names: Novak, David, 1941- author.
Title: God-talk : the heart of Judaism / David Novak.
Description: Lanham, Maryland : Rowman & Littlefield Publishers, 2024. | Includes
  bibliographical references and index.
Identifiers: LCCN 2023041092 (print) | LCCN 2023041093 (ebook) |
  ISBN 9781538187135 (cloth) | ISBN 9781538187142 (paperback) |
  ISBN 9781538187159 (ebook)
Subjects: LCSH: God (Judaism)
Classification: LCC BM610 .N67 2024 (print) | LCC BM610 (ebook) |
  DDC 296.3/11–dc23/eng/20231002
LC record available at https://lccn.loc.gov/2023041092
LC ebook record available at https://lccn.loc.gov/2023041093

To the memory of my revered teacher

Rabbi Louis (Eliezer Aryeh ha-Levi) Finkelstein

"One should learn Torah where one's heart is."
(Babylonian Talmud: Avodah Zarah 19a)

Contents

Preface

It is indisputable that the Jewish tradition—also called Judaism—is permeated by God-talk. That fact alone would justify my writing this book, that is, by attempting to clearly show how God-talk actually operates in some key areas of concern in the Jewish tradition. As such, the subject matter of this book might well be of interest to Jews and non-Jews concerned with how thinkers in the Jewish tradition engage in God-talk intelligently. However, the indispensability of God-talk for the ongoing Jewish tradition has been seriously challenged in modern times, especially quite recently. That impels me to write this book. As somebody actively committed to the ongoing Jewish tradition and its practical and theoretical coherence, my purpose here is to show how God-talk has clearly permeated the tradition heretofore and why God-talk still ought to clearly permeate the ongoing tradition now and hereafter.

My first task is historical, saying some things that are true about Judaism. My second task is philosophical, saying what Judaism itself teaches to be true. Speaking the Torah's truth is an imperative for those properly prepared to do so (see Maimonides, *Sefer ha-Mitsvot*, pos. no. 9) especially when its truth is being publicly denied.

My task here is to speak primarily in a prescriptive voice and secondarily in a descriptive voice. That is, what ought to be said as true by those of us committed to the tradition can now be shown as being consistent with what has been traditionally said as true in the past. That is done not just by representing the tradition accurately and coherently but even more so by speaking its truth in a contemporary idiom, thus enabling the tradition to still speak to perennial human concerns too serious to be permanently repressed. The primacy of the prescriptive voice here means that I (and certainly not I alone) have to speak the truth that ought to be said now. The subsequently descriptive voice here means that what is being said here de novo is not made up ex nihilo.

Now on some key questions of what ought to be said as true, there have been reoccurring debates throughout the Jewish tradition. So if a Jewish thinker wants to still speak prescriptively as a member of the tradition, this person will have to take sides by arguing for the traditional view he or she thinks has a better take on a specific question than do its rivals. Nevertheless, this choice of one view over its rivals should not cause a Jewish thinker to read the rival views or their proponents out of the tradition (see B. Eruvin 13b)—that is, unless that view ignores the rather broad dogmatic boundaries set by the tradition itself (see M. Sanhedrin 10.1). And the most fundamental boundary not to be transgressed is that God-talk lies at the heart of Judaism (see Maimonides, *Mishneh Torah*: Yesodei ha-Torah, 1.1–4).

The challenge to the indispensability of God-talk for the ongoing Jewish tradition, however, has come from the secularist ideology adopted by many modern Jews. There are three types of contemporary Jewish secularism. First, some Jewish thinkers have attempted to radically revise the Jewish tradition so that God-talk is excised from it entirely as if it were never there. Second, other Jewish thinkers have dismantled God-talk by making it designate someone or something far less than the Lord God of Israel. Third, still other Jewish thinkers while recognizing God-talk's centrality in the past as a fact nonetheless maintain that we should supersede God-talk in the present and the future by leaving it behind in the irretrievable past.

Considering the necessary ubiquity of God-talk in the Jewish tradition heretofore, the burden of proof is on those who would coherently constitute a new, secular Judaism without the centrality of God-talk (see B. Baba Kama 46b). But could the subject of such radical surgery survive intact without her heart (see B. Ketubot 46a)? Furthermore, since God-talk is integral to many other traditions and their languages, both Jews and non-Jews will recognize that secular Judaism is the Jewish version of an overall secularist attempt to purge God from the human world by purging God-talk from all our inherited languages, even prohibiting it from now being spoken in the secular space. Therefore I shall try to show that a world from which God-talk has been purged is a world in which the deepest human concerns cannot be dealt with because its inhabitants have lost the words with which to discuss those concerns. Indeed, the challenge here and now is not unique to traditional Judaism even though it must be met in a distinctly Jewish way by committed Jewish thinkers. Arguing against the elimination of God-talk in the secular space is needed to clear the area of public discourse so that God-talk can be retrieved, so that it not let itself be put into a cultural closet.

My primary task, though, is not to engage here in a sustained polemic with those who would amputate the heart of Judaism. At the very least I am aware of their challenge to me and those like me, and by implication they are challenged thereby to show the greater coherence and adequacy of their version of Judaism. Instead, my primary task here is to show that God-talk operates in some of the most important areas of concern in the Jewish tradition; that it is logically coherent and empirically adequate to the traditional Jewish sources; and that it can be spoken intelligently in the present tense in the first-person plural.

The book contains five chapters, two of which have already been published and have now been slightly rewritten. One chapter began as a paper delivered at a conference four years ago. Two chapters were written for this book exclusively. Because all these chapters were written at different times, there is a certain amount of unavoidable repetition of key texts and concepts that wouldn't be the case if this book had been written over a continuous period of time as a monograph.

Here are the chapters of the book with the titles of their subsections to give readers some indication of the topics dealt with in them.

Chapter 1 was written for this volume. The subsections are (1) "Speaking on Strange Ground," (2) "Retrieving God-Talk," (3) God-Talk and Its Critics," (4) Epistemological Dismissal," (5) "Psychological Dismissal," (6) "God-Speakers: A Minority," (7) "Positive Jewish God-Talk," (8) "Covenantal Theology: Divine God-Talk," and (9) "Covenantal Theology: Human God-Talk."

Chapter 2 was originally published under the same title as the lead essay in *The Cambridge Companion to Jewish Theology*. My thanks go to Cambridge University Press for their permission to publish this essay in this volume. The subsections are (1) "Two Views of Jewish Theology," (2) "The Primacy of Revelation," (3) "Halakhah and Aggadah," (4) "Creation, Revelation, and Redemption," (5) "Halakhah and Aggadah at Sinai," (6) "Two Types of Commandments and Their Aggadic Components," (7) and "The Enterprise of Jewish Theology Today."

Chapter 3 began as a paper delivered to a conference of Islamic, Christian, and Jewish thinkers held in the Princeton Theological Seminary in 2019. This chapter is an expansion of that paper. The subsections are (1) "God's Thoughts," (2) "The Metaphysical View of God's Inner and Outer Life," (3) "Kabbalah: Total Divine Inwardness," (4) "Hermann Cohen: Being and Becoming," (5) "The Existential View of God's Inner and Outer Life," (6) "God's Prayer," and (7) "Divine Pathos."

Chapter 4 was written for this volume although it actually began in the class I teach on the weekly Torah reading at Shaarei Shomayim Synagogue, Toronto. The subsections are (1) "Desiring Vision of God," (2) "Is God to Be Seen?" (3) "God's Visibility," (4) "God's Freedom," and (5) "Seeing and Hearing."

Chapter 5 was originally a chapter titled "Natural Law, Natural Theology, and Human Rights in the Jewish Tradition" in *The Cambridge Handbook of Natural Law and Human Rights*. I thank Cambridge University Press for their permission to publish this essay in this volume. The subsections are (1) "Two

Approaches to Natural Law," (2) "Natural Theology: Saadiah Gaon," (3) "Six Questionable Propositions of Natural Theology," (4) "Normative Theology and Natural Law," (5) "Natural Law and Human Rights," (6) "Natural Law and Positive Law," and (7) "Natural Law and Ontology."

This book is the result of a good many conversations over many years. In listing some of my interlocutors while admitting to perhaps having missed some significant names, my apologies are due to them or to their memory. First, my teachers (formal and informal) who influenced my thinking on God-talk. In my early days in Chicago, there were Meyer Goldberg, Curt Peritz, and Harry H. Ruskin. When I was an undergraduate at the University of Chicago (1957–1961), two of my teachers were Markus Barth and Leo Strauss. When I was a rabbinical student at the Jewish Theological Seminary of America (1961–1966), there were Louis Finkelstein, Robert Gordis, David Weiss Halivni, Abraham Joshua Heschel (my theology mentor), Saul Lieberman, Seymour Siegel, and Moses Zucker. And when I was a graduate student at Georgetown University (1966–1971), there were Louis Dupré and Germain Grisez (my philosophy mentor). Second, there have been my students: James A. Diamond, Yaniv Feller, Alexander Green; Martin Kavka, Jonathan Milevsky, Paul Nahme, Randi Rashkover, Dianna Roberts-Zauderer, Cole Sadler, Gregor Scherzinger, Thomas Slabon, Noman Tobias, Robert Tuttle, Alan Verskin. Third, there have been friends and colleagues: Gary Anderson, Jerry Balitsky, Leora Batnitzky, Sholom Eisenstat, Albert Dov Friedberg, Lenn E. Goodman, Adam Hincks, Baruch Frydman-Kohl, Menachem Kellner, Matthew Levering, Shaul Magid, Bruce Marshall, Alan Mittleman, Morris Moskovitch, Richard John Neuhaus, Peter Ochs, Abdulaziz Sachedina, R. Kendall Soulen, Sol Tanenzapf, Asher Turin, and Robert Louis Wilken. With all of these good people, each in their own way, I have been blessed by their conversation due to their willingness to teach me many precious things about God and God's creation. "From all those who have taught me I have gained insight" (Psalms 119:99).

It is a great pleasure to work with Richard Brown and his colleagues at Rowman & Littlefield. When he was at Georgetown University Press, Richard edited my 2007 book *The Sanctity of Human Life*. I very much appreciate his encouragement and wise counsel then and now. I also gratefully remember a book I edited, *Jerusalem and Athens Revisited: Leo Strauss and Judaism*, that was so well published by Rowman & Littlefield.

This book is dedicated to the memory of my revered teacher Rabbi Louis Finkelstein. The greatness of the Jewish Theological Seminary of America during his reign as chancellor (1940–1972) was largely due to his inspired and inspiring leadership. This dedication is my way of showing my gratitude to him for accepting me, teaching me, and guiding me as a student and as a graduate of "the Seminary." Indeed, one of the great honors of my life is the foreword to my first book, *Law and Theology in Judaism*, that he graciously wrote.

Finally and most importantly, my thanks to God for giving me enough strength of body and mind, in this my eighty-second year, to still engage in what are truly God's "wondrous testimonies" (Psalms 119:129).

Toronto
Tammuz 5783
June 2023

Chapter 1

Introduction

Speaking on Strange Ground

"How [*aikh*] can we sing the Lord's song [*shir adonai*] on strange ground?" (Psalms 137:4). So sang the Jewish exiles in Babylonia after their deportation from Jerusalem in the wake of the destruction of the Temple in 586 BCE (where the psalms were sung during the sacrificial service).[1] What are the exiles saying here? Are they uttering an exclamation, or are they asking a question? If this is an exclamation, it might be in effect saying, "No, we can't sing the Lord's song in a foreign country because the words of our sacred song can't be translated into the words of the foreign country's language."[2] On the other hand, if this is a question, the answer might be "Yes, we can sing the Lord's song there but we need to know *how* to sing our song authentically in this foreign language so it might be understood here." This answer also implies that the new language is not only the native language spoken by the Gentiles among themselves, not only the language the Jews have to speak to the Gentiles among whom they are presently living, but even the language the Jews are presently speaking among themselves.

Now the term the "Lord's song" can connote Jewish "God-talk" (whether sung, spoken, or even written) in general. By "God-talk" I mean (1) what God says to humans of Godself in biblical revelation; (2) what humans can theologically speculate of Godself; and (3) what Jewish tradition mandates humans can say to God of themselves in prayer.

Interpreting the words of the psalm above as an exclamation and then having them connote Jewish God-talk in general means that Jewish God-talk must be confined to inter-Jewish discourse and that conducting Jewish God-talk elsewhere is like the sacrilege of offering a sacrifice outside the Temple precincts.[3] On the other hand, interpreting the words of the psalm above as a genuine query and then having them connote Jewish God-talk in general implies a positive answer: "Yes, Jewish God-talk can be conducted in a foreign language." Nevertheless, that language must have the capacity for

1

Jewish God-talk to be authentically expressed therein without distorting its essential meaning. Some languages have that capacity; others do not.[4] Of those languages not having this capacity, some never had it; others had it but lost it or they had it but the words that had been adequate for Jewish God-talk (or any God-talk) were removed from public discourse by deliberate efforts to secularize the language.

In today's secular milieu, God-talk has been steadily removed, indeed banished, from public discourse. Some Jews accept that removal as a fait accompli. They opt to either abandon the secular cultural milieu because any God-talk is not welcome there (and where they don't want to be anyway), or they opt to abandon God-talk altogether because they want to be welcome in the secular milieu even if that means giving up the God-talk lying at the heart of the Jewish tradition.

On the other hand, the removal of God-talk from public discourse is not accepted as a fait accompli by other Jews. We want to conduct our God-talk in public discourse wherever we happen to be but with theological integrity, neither fleeing into an intellectual ghetto nor obsequiously subordinating ourselves to another culture. Like the question (rather than the exclamation) of those in the psalm genuinely inquiring and thus truly searching for a positive answer, our question becomes "How do we conduct our Jewish God-talk in a secular cultural milieu where God-speakers are a distinct minority?" How can this to be done, steering clear of the Scylla of sectarianism and the Charybdis of assimilation?

How can Jews (or Christians or Muslims for that matter) conduct their traditional God-talk in a cultural milieu from which the public discourse of God-talk has been largely—indeed intentionally—eliminated? This book answers "Yes you can" to this genuine question. Here I attempt to explain Jewish God-talk in and for our contemporary, secular, cultural milieu by first arguing that God-talk has not, indeed cannot, be eliminated from contemporary public discourse. In fact, attempts at this elimination have and still do greatly impoverish the historic languages from which even their specialized intellectual discourse has been abstracted. Indeed, those who speak this abstract dialect still cannot dispense with their need as communicating beings to speak with other persons the more comprehensive language they have inherited from their cultural forbearers in a culture they didn't invent. God-talk is an integral component of that prior, more comprehensive language. God-talk cannot be excised from interpersonal public communication any more than that prior language in its fullness can be excised from current public discourse.

RETRIEVING GOD-TALK

Due to semi-successful attempts by militant atheists to eliminate God-talk from public discourse, however, the historic language of the culture—and especially its God-talk—needs to be retrieved. That needs to be done so God-speakers can speak again in public in a language that can no longer be silenced for being irretrievably passé, like some embarrassing, primitive ancestor. Also, by retrieving public Jewish God-talk, Jews can actually help others retrieve the God-talk taken away from them too by those who believe they can reinvent language altogether so as to conform to their own political-cultural agenda. This retrieval can be done by uncovering a vocabulary still employed by religious Jews, Christians, and Muslims that can still be cogently employed when speaking of and to God in public. As such, I happily appreciate both parallel and common efforts to make God-talk truly intelligible universally.[5]

That a language has the capacity for God-talk to be conducted therein is a possible meaning of the rabbinic principle "The Torah speaks according to human language (*ke-lashon bnei adam*)."[6] Now that could be saying that the Torah—the source of all authentic Jewish God-talk—is given in language already being spoken in the world.[7] And whereas God created the cosmos out of nothing (ex nihilo), there being nothing to precede it, God gave the Torah de novo. That is, although God gave the Torah newly into the world, the world was already there, and humans already had multiple languages they had already been speaking beforehand. What the old words—especially the name "God"—mean, and what people believed were their real referents, God now revealed in the Torah that these words are true.[8] It was like the old words were waiting for God to let people know that what they had heretofore only believed to be true was now confirmed to be the truth by their experience of the event of revelation and their acceptance of its message.[9] However, nobody could accept statements about God and from God to be true unless they understood what the name "God" means.

In order for the Torah and its God-talk to be understood by the speakers of a human language to whom the Torah is given, their language must have the vocabulary whereby the Torah's God-talk could be expressed.[10] But if a language is devoid of words and concepts adequate for the expression of God-talk, the Torah's truth would then be blocked from being revealed as it would fall on deaf ears. "They have ears, but they do not hear" (Jeremiah 5:25).[11] As such, the Torah's truth coming down from heaven would have no place to land on earth.[12]

GOD-TALK AND ITS CRITICS

In this book I attempt to explain to both religious and secular readers that the God-talk Jewish thinkers have spoken and still do speak is cogent, having a logic governing what can be said and what cannot be said correctly, and that it draws upon rich resources in the Jewish tradition accurately. My explication of Jewish God-talk here attempts to show how it can be spoken cogently. And since philosophy seems to be the most precise and insightful way of examining how humans speak of questions of deepest concern, it is employed here. I hope to indicate how some of the basic questions regarding human language, in which God-talk is inextricably embedded, are discussed by Western philosophers in ways similar to how they have been discussed in the Jewish tradition.

Before exposing, analyzing, and speculating in earnest on some major themes in Jewish God-talk, there is a need to argue against dismissal of the enterprise to which I am existentially committed as somebody living and working in a tradition that is so saturated with God-talk. That needs to be done because the dismissal of God-talk is ubiquitous in our secular culture and especially in academic discourse, where there seems to be an aversion to any God-talk at all.

In this book I refuse the attempt of atheists to keep those of us who sincerely speak the name "God" out of public discourse, shoving us into the closet as it were.[13] Alas, this can only be done polemically by arguing against the rationale of their dismissals of God-talk and those of us who speak it publicly in the present tense. Nevertheless, this book is not essentially a polemic. The polemic here is but a ground-clearing exercise so as to enable me to get to the book's positive thesis quickly yet as carefully as possible. This cannot be done cogently if one tries to do an end run around very serious attempts to block God-speakers from speaking in public at all. The opposition of many atheists to authentic God-talk being conducted in a cultural milieu they believe they own is often quite vehement. It should never be underestimated.

Atheistic dismissal of God-talk is twofold. It either attempts to dismiss God-talk altogether as nonsense or it attempts to show that when the name "God" is invoked, it actually names some other reality that its speakers have now forgotten having long ago repressed their memory of it. In this latter view, speakers of their common language who still invoke the name "God" do so because they are now unconscious of their own wish-projection, whose product is their fantastic invention of a god. Thus it is advocated that those who have now become enlightened or conscious of this illusion can—indeed they should—overcome it by working through it and that they should encourage others less enlightened to act similarly.

Both of these atheistic views, despite their specific differences, generally deny that anybody can speak cogently of the extramental reality that religious people call God. These dismissals need to be countered by those of us God-speakers who do not accept the banishment of God-talk from current public discourse. This must be done by showing how these dismissals of God-talk are part of—perhaps the reason for—modern attempts to impoverish ordinary language to the point where what could be expressed in the past can no longer be expressed in the present. The task of perspicacious God-speakers, who have not been intimidated by this imposed deprivation of the common cultural-linguistic heritage, is to retrieve the intelligibility of what has been relegated to the intellectual dustbin of meaninglessness. In our case, God-talk needs to be retrieved by first arguing that its banishment has been arbitrary and then by showing what it is and how it can be done again intelligently.[14]

EPISTEMOLOGICAL DISMISSAL

The first dismissal of God-talk we might call epistemological. Its error is that it confines all meaningful speech to its own invented, descriptive language. Anything that is not verifiable is what cannot be spoken of, the prime example being any talk of God.[15] However, by confining meaningful speech to verifiable descriptions of impersonal entities or things only, thus eliminating anything normative from it, those who hold the narrower view of language thereby dismiss most of what historical languages contain out of hand. By so doing, proponents of this view are certainly myopic, being unwilling to accept the fact that normative human speech is unavoidable and that normative speech is primarily prescriptive and only secondarily descriptive. In fact, it could be argued that our descriptions of things are ultimately for the sake of knowing how they can be used effectively in fulfilling prescriptive claims made to us by other persons with whom we are interrelated in a common enterprise. Only persons are the subjects and objects of normative speech. So for example, scientists learn to speak correctly about the things they observe in order to answer (or at least respond to) a question posed to them by their fellow scientists with whom they are engaged in the communal discourse that is science.[16]

Furthermore, even if God-talk is not a topic for discussion in strictly scientific discourse, it is still an important component in the ordinary language of the larger society where scientists too have to speak with their nonscientific fellow members. As such, scientists can abstract their discourse from ordinary language so that it pertains only to observable entities and their quantification, but they may not go further by excising from ordinary language those components that they cannot as scientists deal with. When that is done, however, whether by scientists themselves or by intellectuals on their behalf, we are left with scientism, presuming that what cannot be spoken of in scientific discourse therefore does not exist.

All interpersonal discourse, no matter how informal, consists of the claims of those speaking with one another, making claims upon one another. But from whom does a member of a normatively ordered society derive his or her right to claim any other member of that society or the society itself? This is an important question, requiring an answer when one's right to make a claim is challenged. At such challenging times, the question often is "Who gave you the right to claim X from Y?" If one answers that his or her right is an entitlement from society, then this person has no claim on that society itself, which often attempts to recall what it had previously given to individual members. In fact, often the most unjust claims made upon a member of a society are made when the society unjustly entitles itself or unjustly privileges some members of the society over other members of the society.

However, to say "I gave myself this right" means "I have created myself as a normative being." That is as absurd as saying "I have created myself as a natural being."[17] Therefore, humans have come to ascribe their rights to a transcendent source of all rights and the commanded duties corresponding to them. That is the case whether these rights and duties devolve on the society or on its individual members. This source is the creator of the very existence of the society and its individual members. They are both coequally creatures of the same creator. As such, an individual has no priority over his or her society any more than a society has priority over its members. Their interrelationship is dialectical. One's society was there before its individual members came into this world and will probably continue after they depart from this world. Yet that priority is overturned by the fact that individual persons have the ability to leave their native society (either physically or by repudiating its moral authority over them while still having to remain there physically), or to join another society, or to found a new society, or to survive the demise of their native society elsewhere. God, however, has priority over both society and its individual members since God transcends them both whereas they cannot transcend God.[18] That is so even when they think they have killed God, whether collectively or individually.

Even though this is where moral and political discourse becomes metaphysical, necessarily involving God-talk, it is not abstract philosophical discourse only to be conducted in an arcane academic milieu. It is, in fact, assumed in ordinary moral judgment, conducted in ordinary language.[19] So for example, when we condemn somebody for being authoritarian, which is the illegitimate usurpation of proper authority, we often denounce this person as a charlatan for "playing God." Thus we say to him or her, "Who do you think you are, God?" That objection assumes that God truly exists, that the name "God" has a real referent, and that the person being condemned is "not *really* God at all!" But if it were not assumed that God exists, would there be any point in denouncing somebody for impersonating someone who we believe is a phantom?

The metaphysical dimension of any normative language, and the normative order it constitutes, enables God-speakers to speak the name "God" with its proper meaning wherever that language is allowed to be spoken in its fullness. Of course this doesn't prove God exists. It only argues that living under a normative order is a necessity for humans as political beings. And to affirm that order's authority at least implies the recognition of the transcendent originator and sustainer of that order, which is expressed in the ordinary language spoken by the members of this normative order. Nevertheless, this recognition does not require one to attempt to argue persons into believing or having faith in the lawgiver who commands but is not himself commanded. One can only argue for the plausibility that there is an irreducible source of a normative order and that the ultimate authority of that order could only be the Creator-God.[20] Anyone else claiming that ultimate authority is easily exposed to be a false god whose claims are idolatrous.

Atheists who deny God is real and who are convinced that all God-talk is nonsense should not speak the name "God" at all. Nevertheless, they have no good reason to try to remove from public discourse those who do correctly invoke the name "God" even if they themselves believe these God-speakers are fantasizing. Yet all too often atheists have the political power (like Lenin, Stalin, and Mao) to prohibit God-talk altogether and punish those who do engage in it sincerely. That is because traditional God-talk is a great threat to the absolute that they have inevitably replaced God with. That replacement is inevitable because they certainly have to speak in a normative language constituting a normative order, which cannot fully function without superlatives. This was stated most poignantly by T. S. Eliot to a largely secular audience in Cambridge University in 1939 on the eve of World War II.

> The term "democracy," as I have said again and again, does not contain enough positive content to stand alone against the forces you dislike—it can easily be transformed by them. If you will not have God (and He is a jealous God) you should pay your respects to Hitler or Stalin.[21]

PSYCHOLOGICAL DISMISSAL

The second dismissal of God-talk we might call psychological.[22] God-speakers can retort to this dismissal of God-talk as follows: You seem to think that

God-talk was introduced into public discourse as a novum by those who forgot whom they were really intending to speak of in the first place. So what might be called their God-illusion is by now their unconscious substitution of what they have forgotten.[23] But if the name "God" is the name of someone new whom nobody in their discursive world had ever heard of before, why then would anybody believe the name to have a real referent (much less have any authority, which is what any god has) as opposed to being a fanciful projection?[24] The name "God" would only be intelligible to those already speaking that name and believing that it names a reality they themselves did not invent.

The psychological dismissal of God-talk presumes there was a time when humans were not religious, when the name "God" had never been heard in the human world. The burden of proof, though, is on those who presume that humans were once without any God-talk intending a real, not a humanly invented, referent. But that requires locating a time and a place when human God-talk was introduced, which can only be a guess based on the kind of wishful thinking the psychological dismissal of God-talk itself claims to have deconstructed.

Conversely, those who hold the more traditional view that God-talk is coeval with human existence do not have to prove a beginning in history that has not been convincingly shown to have ever actually occurred. It is easier to assume that God-talk is coeval with humans emerging in the world as necessarily normative-linguistic beings.[25] The burden of proof is on those who say otherwise. Nevertheless, the strength of the psychological dismissal of God-talk is that its proponents are still able to take two historical facts seriously that proponents of the epistemological dismissal of God-talk simply ignore, treating God-talk as if it never had been conducted intelligently at all.

Proponents of the psychological dismissal of God-talk, being more historically sensitive, are able to take seriously the fact that many speakers of the natural languages in which public discourse is inextricably rooted still authentically invoke the name "God," intending by this invocation that God is real and not just a figment of their imagination. As such, those who hold this psychological dismissal are at least able to respect the intelligence of the many smart people (even philosophers) who have spoken and still do speak the name "God," thereby intending a reality outside their own minds that they couldn't have invented. In other words, those laboring under this illusion are not taken to be stupid. Their illusion is not cognitive but emotional. Their illusion is not due to what they don't know; it is due to what they want and wish for. So what they need in order to overcome this illusion is not arguments but therapy. That therapy is not conducted through philosophical argument but rather through psychological introspection.

Nevertheless, at least with the epistemological deniers of God-talk, a reasoned public dialogue is still possible. But the psychological deniers of God-talk will only engage in the private discourse of psychotherapist and patient. Unlike the still possible publicly reasoned public dialogue between God-speakers and atheistic deniers as equal partners in a common enterprise, in the sequestered discourse of patient to psychotherapist and psychotherapist to patient, the therapist-patient relationship is unequal. Therapists are the interpreters of the emotional data patients bring to them for insight into their real motives, which the patients cannot provide themselves with. Theirs is not a dialogue appealing to common reasons pertaining to them both equally.

GOD-SPEAKERS: A MINORITY

Both kinds of dismissal of God-talk, however, seem to be less vehement and less persuasive now than they once were. Yet that might be because many people in our secular cultural milieu believe these two dismissals have already accomplished their task of removing God-talk from public discourse. Hence there no longer seems to be any need for these dismissals to be reiterated again by arguing for them. That is why the task of God-speakers is to get God-deniers to pose their arguments against us seriously again so that we might counter them with equal seriousness. But that only can be done when discerning God-speakers are able to deconstruct the arguments made against us. This negating or polemical task gives us the opening to have our positive God-talk get at least a tolerant hearing in the contemporary secular milieu where public discourse is conducted.

In premodern times when God-talk was ubiquitous, it was the deniers who had to argue for their inclusion in public discourse. Now the burden of argumentation is on the God-speakers. That is because in premodern times, God-speakers were the vast majority and God-deniers were a small minority even in the more intellectual areas of the culture. Today, however, it is the reverse. God-speakers are the minority and God-deniers (or at least those indifferent to God-talk altogether) are the majority and especially in the more powerful areas of culture-formation like the universities, the courts, and the media. It is always the minority, not the majority, in any culture who have to argue for their right to speak in public discourse. Today this requires perspicacious God-speakers to argue persuasively that God-talk cannot be dismissed. And more importantly, it requires our showing insightfully how God-talk has been done and is still being done cogently today and that various God-speakers are entitled to claim an attentive hearing in a truly pluralistic secular space, that is, even by those who do not want to enter into our God-talk themselves or by those who insist their kind of God-talk is the only legitimate God-talk to be heard in public.

Nevertheless, some atheists today consciously and willingly avoid speaking of God (which means the one and only God proclaimed by Jewish, Christian, and Islamic monotheism) altogether. Instead, they only speak of gods or a god. That is their way of avoiding the normative meaning of monotheistic God-talk let alone whether it is true or not. However, as we have just noted, they do so as what might be the raison d'être of their impoverishing the historical language of their culture that is still spoken outside their limited discursive circle.

Finally, by not trying to prove the existence of the universal God of whom Jewish God-speakers speak, or by trying to prove the truth of the particular event of God's revelation in which Jews traditionally have faith that God spoke to us, I am not trying here to get others to join us by speaking God-talk like we do or speaking God-talk at all. Our speaking the name "God" in public is not a proselytizing project. Here I am only trying to show that our invoking in public the name "God" is not nonsense, that it has meaning, and that our invocation of it is to show others where our primary existential commitment lies. Nevertheless, its truth must "come from another place" (Esther 4:14).

POSITIVE JEWISH GOD-TALK

We are now ready to discuss what Jewish God-talk is and the theological perspective that I think is more cogent than the alternatives and more adequately corresponds to the biblical-rabbinic tradition than do the alternatives. Let me say at the outset, though, this is not a zero-sum game. That is, I do not say what I think is true and therefore what others think is false. It is not an either-or proposition. Rather, I would suggest my preferred perspective is more cogent and more adequate to the sources than are the alternatives. Nevertheless, by my stating the alternatives to my preferred perspective as fairly and as empathetically as possible, readers might find these alternatives more cogent and more adequately related to the Jewish tradition than my own preference. That is a chance I am willing to take.

There are four theoretical perspectives Jewish theologians have employed for engaging in God-talk: (1) natural theology, (2) metaphysical theology, (3) kabbalistic theology, and (4) what can be called covenantal theology. Regarding these four theological perspectives—which are discussed at length and in depth in the chapters of this book—by way of introduction let me comment on them while indicating which one I prefer and thus employ in this book.

First, from the perspective of natural theology, we humans can speak *about* God, but humans can neither speak directly *of* God nor speak directly *to* God. And God speaks neither of us nor to us. Here God is silent. It is we humans who speak about God wisely making the cosmos, yet human speech about God does not come out of our direct experience of God's creative activity (after all, no humans were present to witness the dawn of creation). Natural theology talks about God as cosmic artificer by inference, that is, by seeing in nature an analogy to our own artistic creations. This is what has been called the "argument from design."[26] This argument states that we know from our experience that intricate artifacts clearly indicate they have been intentionally designed or ordered to be what they are. Since natural entities are more intricately designed than are humanly made things, we can infer that they have been so designed by an artificer much greater than ourselves. Thus what is true of humanly made artifacts is, all the more so, true of natural entities.

In scripture, conversely, before humans can speak to God or of God, God first speaks *to* humans (Genesis 2:16–17). The first human to speak *to* God was Adam, the first human person, whose power of speech was because God spoke to Adam first, demanding that Adam answer God's question "Where are you?" (Genesis 3:19).[27] The first human person to speak *of* God was Abraham (Genesis 24:3), whom God had invited to speak to him (Genesis 18:17–33), and who was the person God had previously spoken to (Genesis 12:1–4; 15:1–16).[28]

From the perspective of natural theology, though, we humans do not speak to God any more than God speaks to us. As such, there can't be a direct relation to someone to whom we do not speak and who does not speak to us. The most we can do is admire the divine artificer when contemplating nature, but we cannot infer from nature that its artificer actually speaks to us, demanding that we listen to him or that he wants to listen to us. That is why natural theology cannot be an adequate explanation of what is meant by "religion" (minimally, meaning Judaism, Christianity, and Islam), which is a direct, two-way relationship between God and humans and humans and God. This relationship involves God speaking to humans through revelation, and humans speaking to God through prayer.

Now both revelation and prayer are basically prescriptive, involving claims and counterclaims. Through verbal revelation God claims human obedience to his commandments by addressing them to us; and through verbal worship or prayer we humans claim God's answer to our pleas by addressing them to God. Natural theology, though, is descriptive and thus unable to explain the normative content of religion. In fact, it cannot even prepare us for normative religion any more than knowing what is the case can then lead to doing what ought to be done.[29] It could be said that natural theology is aesthetic rather than essentially religious. At best, aesthetics is tangential to religion. Aesthetics only becomes a religious activity when one appreciates the beauty of God's creation and thanks God for the opportunity to behold it and enjoy it.[30]

Second, from the perspective of metaphysical theology, God speaks of Godself—what God is—in a way we humans can intuit. We thereby differentiate our imperfect, becoming selves from God as the perfect being who never had to become what he already is eternally. That limits any idolatrous pretension by making our difference from God one of kind. All the more so, that limits any pretension to equate ourselves with God.

Now affirming God's being also means God is necessarily relative to the existent cosmos, which is contingent on God. So when we humans infer from our creaturely imperfection our dependence on the most perfect God, we then aspire to become as much like God's perfection as is possible for fallible humans in our very imperfect world. This aspiration is expressed in speech and in action. In that way, human aspiration to be like God translates into prescribed speech and deed (*mitsvot*). Nevertheless, this relation is not an interrelationship; rather, it is a one-way relation. That is, we know how to relate ourselves to God but we don't know how God relates Godself to us. In fact, we don't know how or even whether God is with us. So metaphysical theology does not enable humans to speak positively of the interrelationship of God and humans, what the Bible calls "the covenant" (*ha-berit*).[31] Yet this is the central theme in biblical revelation, the locus of all authentic Jewish God-talk. At best, metaphysics is tangential to God-talk, speculating on the implications of revealed God-talk. But when metaphysics is presumed to ground God-talk, it only grounds God-talk coming from a place other than Sinai.

Third, from the perspective of kabbalistic theology, the Torah is God totally speaking of Godself and nothing else. And since the Torah is coequal with all reality, nothing outside it truly exists at all as there is nothing outside God at all. Everything takes place within God. Moreover, human action mandated by the divine Torah is not the action of beings separate from God. Human action is essentially conscious participation in what is a complete, inner divine reality. Even when a Torah-mandated act seems to be a mundane human deed, it is really a participation in the inner divine reality (*elohut*). And even when not immediately evident, the essential function of this mandated act is symbolic, pointing to what is ultimately true of the divine life.

However, there can be no interrelationship between those who are not separate from each other any more than a part can relate with the whole that encompasses it or that the whole can relate with a part inside it. There is no externality here, which is presupposed by any interrelationship. Such a divine-human interrelationship is only possible when the creator is separate from his creatures and creatures are separate from their creator. Thus in biblical revelation, God speaks of Godself in relation to humans with whom God has an ongoing, covenantal, interrelationship. Jewish God-talk is the expression of this real interrelationship. It is an interrelationship through which God who is not human and humans who are not God come together. Yet God doesn't absorb us humans into Godself any more than we humans could absorb God into ourselves.

All these objections make kabbalistic God-talk problematic theologically.

Finally, we come to the fourth perspective, that of covenantal theology, by which I think Jewish God-talk is most cogently and most adequately explained.

COVENANTAL THEOLOGY: DIVINE GOD-TALK

The original and ever prime locus of all authentic Jewish God-talk is biblical revelation. This revelation being verbal is essentially normative: eliciting an active response to its call to listen to it then prescribing what we humans are to do in response. In one way or another, biblical revelation is God addressing us humans by making claims on us, to which we are to dutifully respond in word and in deed. Thus the most foundational commandment in the Torah, given to us at the beginning of the Decalogue (the Ten Commandments) is directly normative: "I am the Lord your God" (Exodus 20:2). God speaks here immediately in the first person singular, addressing Godself to humans immediately in the second person singular.[32]

The commandments follow upon the people's general acceptance of what has been revealed, namely, God's wise and beneficent kingship. They are further specifications of God's wisdom and benevolence.[33] The commandments wisely and beneficently guide the people in their active journey through this world, directing them to their final destination, what the rabbis term "the world-yet-to-come" (*ha'olam ha-ba*).[34] Only then are we humans, who have been so addressed by God, able to keep the commandments freely rather than coercively, happily rather than grudgingly. This acceptance, called "faith" (*emunah*), also dispels the suspicion that the commandments were given to harm us. Yet more needs to be told so that we humans addressed by God can willingly accept God's commandments because they are wise and beneficial.[35]

Descriptive God-talk is what is needed to narrate for us the context in which God's commandments, the content of revelation, are given and received. That context is the covenantal relationship between God and the people Israel, concretized at the event of the Sinaitic revelation of the Torah. Thus in the second clause of the foundational commandment, God proclaims he is the one "who took you out of the land of Egypt, out of the house of bondage." This clause describes what the people had recently experienced, namely, being taken out of Egypt.[36] Moreover, even this description of God's taking Israel out of Egypt is actually a description of God's fulfilling a previous prescription, which God autonomously made to Godself. It states that God did what he promised to do, that is, what God autonomously commanded Godself to do in a covenantal oath. "I remember My covenant (*beriti*). Therefore, say to the Israelites I am the Lord, who *shall* take you out from under the burdens of Egypt" (Exodus 6:5–6). In other words, God is telling or describing to the people that he has fulfilled his promise to them made previously.

Accepting the commandments because God's authority over us ("I am the Lord your God") is unavoidable means that we accept them due to our being in awe (*yir'ah*) of God's power over us. Accepting the commandments because God's benevolence to us ("who took you out of the land of Egypt") is irresistible means we accept them due to our being in love (*ahavah*) with God.[37]

Subsequent God-talk is conducted by theologians inferring from these biblical narrations of what God did why God did it. And subsequent to that, some theologians can and do speculate as to how God deliberates over which of the possible options to be realized as wise and benevolent action God chooses to do with God's human creatures, who have the unique capacity to interrelate with God.

That speculation, however, does not lend itself to any totalizing theological system from whose ideas the narrated events in scripture are but instantiations. Instead, whatever ideas one draws from the biblical narrative are only the result of random, unsystematic reflections on the implications of the biblical narrative itself. In fact, devising a total theological system might well tempt us to deduce revelation and its content from it. But that would turn revelation into a conclusion rather than a datum. That is why the philosophic method best suited for theological inference and speculation is phenomenology.[38] Phenomenological reflection begins with what the data (what we have been given to reflect on) show us. In the case of the Torah's verbal revelation, phenomenological reflection begins with what the Torah is saying to us, that is, what the Torah is giving to us and what we can take from it. (Revelation is called by the rabbis *mattan torah*, "the gift of the Torah."[39]) Since this theological speculation is usually random, imaginative, and often quite tentatively connected to particular biblical texts, it seems to be more akin to the halakhic casuistry one finds in the Talmud and in the responsa literature than it is to the architectonic classification one finds in the medieval law codes. It seems more akin to the often impressionist method one finds in rabbinic midrash, which is why rabbinic midrash provides the best models for Jewish theological speculation.

Whereas descriptive God-talk concerns our experience of what God does for our covenantal relationship with God, prescriptive God-talk is concerned with what we humans ourselves ought to do for our covenantal relationship with God. The former concerns our experience of God's action; the latter concerns God commanding human action.

Prescriptive God-talk consists primarily of the norms God directly commands us humans to do. As for the actual interpretation and application of the primary revealed norms, human authorities have considerable leeway to do what seems right in their eyes.[40] Speculative God-talk (which is theological reflection) goes beyond prescriptive God-talk by conjecturing what it intends, having even more leeway. And what needs to be conjectured from prescriptive God-talk are the reasons God might have employed for specifically commanding humans to do what we have been commanded to do (*ta'amei ha-mitsvot*).[41]

Now some of these reasons are more evident than others and are thus rather easily inferred.[42] When we think these reasons are likely to be God's wise and beneficent purposes in commanding us as God does, our keeping of the commandments becomes our participation in God's governance of the cosmos. It is not just mundane pragmatic action.[43] This can make us more enthusiastic in keeping the commandments as persons created in the image of God. When our intention in keeping the commandments seems to comport with God's intention in giving them to us, we no longer keep God's commandments, which become like "human precepts (*mitsvat anashim*) learned by rote" (Isaiah 29:13). In this case, we keep the commandments because we want to be in harmony with God's wise and beneficent commanding us to keep them and not just because we have to keep them. But when we cannot even think of a probable reason why God commanded us to do or not do a certain act, we have to do even what we don't want to do.[44]

Furthermore, when the authorities charged with interpreting and applying the commandments understand the reasons for which the commandments are prescribed, they have greater insight into how to enhance observance of the commandments and how to reinterpret the commandments when needed.[45] Usually the success of this reinterpretation only requires the jurisprudence of ordinary jurists, who have the wisdom to judge whether a norm whose application is being changed through reinterpretation is practically feasible or not.[46] Now this could well be a political requirement in any ordinary, humanly constructed legal system. But Jewish law (halakhah) doesn't present itself as ordinary jurisprudence. Instead, it presents itself as the humanly formulated structure of the commandments revealed by God in the Torah. Although it couldn't be an actual requirement that halakhists be inspired (let alone be able) to speculate on God's ultimate purposes in legislating in even seemingly mundane matters, it is a desideratum nonetheless. In fact, this speculative God-talk has been impressively engaged in by some sages who are jurists but also theologians.[47]

About some of the less-evident reasons of the commandments, we can only speculate very tentatively if at all. Some of the reasons, about which any speculation could only be guesswork at best, might never be known by us. We can only believe that they are truly in God's mind although this would seem to be forever beyond our ken, at least in this world, being just too arcane for us here and now. But surely God always knows precisely why he commanded us to do all the commandments the way God has commanded us in the Torah to do them. Thus human action realizes divine purposes in cooperation with God whether we humans know these purposes and how they will be ultimately fulfilled or not. In other words, the commandments should always be done willingly even if not always knowingly. And we should at least hope to know, perhaps in the world-yet-to-come, what these reasons truly are.[48]

Finally, the highest level of keeping the commandments is when we discern how God himself performs the acts that have been revealed to us as imitable. They are the acts that God performs in an exemplary manner. As such, we discern God's modus operandi. Therefore, we not only keep the commandments because God commanded them, and not only because of why God commanded them, but because we can imitate how God acts for us exemplarily, which is what we can now do among ourselves in imitation of God.[49]

COVENANTAL THEOLOGY: HUMAN GOD-TALK

So far our representation of Jewish God-talk has been discussing descriptions of what God does with the human recipients of revelation and prescriptions of what these human recipients ought to do with God accordingly. We now need to discuss the kind of Jewish God-talk in which humans speak to God. Liturgy or sacred worship (*avodat ha-qodesh*) is where Jewish God-talk is conducted most extensively, which is in prayer (*tefillah*) as sacred worship's essential verbal component.[50] We now need to look at how speaking to God in prayer is constituted normatively.

Prayer, according to rabbinic tradition, is to be conducted in two ways: (1) by acknowledging the good God has done for us in the past (*hoda'ah*); and (2) by requesting that God do good for us in the future (*baqashah*).[51] The former is looking back from our present vantage point; the latter is looking ahead from our present vantage point. Now this acknowledgment is thankfully remembering the one who benefited us in the past. It is not passive nostalgia. We actively call upon God to remember his past beneficence so that we can reasonably hope that this same divine benefactor will do this same kind of good for us in the future.[52] As such, prayer involves our making a twofold, active appeal to God by reminding God of his past beneficence and, simultaneously, asking God to be benevolent to us again in the future.[53] Our human action, however, is always in the present. It is only from our present vantage point that we remember the past and hope for the future. This past- and future-looking perspective makes the significance of our present action more than ephemeral.

What is the relation of *hoda'ah* and *baqashah*? Do we first request that our needs be fulfilled, only thereafter acknowledging God to be the one to whom our request is to be directed because of what God has done for us in the past? Or do we acknowledge God first, only thereafter requesting that our needs be fulfilled by God? This question is debated in the Talmud, where two rabbis differ over the proper sequence in the liturgy.[54] Rabbi Eliezer holds that we are to request that our needs be fulfilled first, and then acknowledge God. Conversely, Rabbi Joshua holds that we acknowledge God first, thereafter requesting that our needs be fulfilled. Their debate is legal, exegetical, and ultimately theological.

As for the legally structured order (*seder*) of the liturgy, Rabbi Joshua's view is the norm.[55] Logically this makes sense. The rabbis want worshippers to acknowledge exactly whom they are beseeching before actually doing so. In terms of our experience, though, it seems that the expression of our needs by crying out to anyone to fulfill them precedes our acknowledging to whom this expression is to be ultimately directed.[56] In fact, the way we are to pray we learn from Hannah, the mother of the prophet Samuel, who prayed spontaneously out of the depths of her sorrow at being unable to conceive a child (I Samuel 1:10).[57] And her prayer was uttered before any official verbal liturgy had been formulated. In her day, sacrifice was the only kind of official worship. Nevertheless, although spontaneous prayer is still to be done, even encouraged, the rabbis instituted officially composed prayers and the times when they are to be said.[58] And while spontaneous prayer is instituted by individual humans, communal prayer is instituted by the leaders of the community for the members of the community.[59] In other words, humans themselves institute that they are to address God and then how they are to address God.[60] From their communal experience, the members of the community know to whom they are to pray before actually making their requests.[61]

The very act of requesting anything begins in our infancy when we cry out to anyone else, begging them to mercifully save us and nurture us any way possible. This infantile helplessness accompanies us throughout our life as the necessary initiating motivation of our asking anyone else for anything good for ourselves or at least to pay attention to our beseeching them. However, this infantile motive is not a sufficient reason for our making a justifiable claim on anyone else. So as we mature we need to learn from our past experience what is truly good for us, who can be trusted to benefit us, and who we hope will do good for us again in the future.

Thereafter we have to patiently learn how to justify our requests as being reasonable because we deserve what is being requested. That is not because of what we have done—it is not payment for our having done good for our benefactors—but rather it is because of who we are, which is how God has made us (for example, minor children deserve the support of their parents ipso facto and parents deserve the respect and attention of their adult children ipso facto[62]). Thus what begins as our ever-present infantile cries for mercy become more and more our requests for justice. We learn to do that as we progressively attain the language in which to argue for our justifiable claims on those who we trust will respond to them mercifully.

Now when praying becomes an adult exercise, our requests are for more justice than we could expect from any human authority.[63] Although we may always call upon God to act favorably toward us, our requests are just when we can present reasons before God for God to act mercifully toward us. Thus prayer enables us to make a justifiable claim on God, the God whose benefi-cent deeds for us are described in biblical revelation (indeed, were it not for that revelation, we wouldn't know them at all). The descriptive biblical nar-rative enables us to know it is to God alone that our greatest requests are to be made, requests that should not be made to anyone else because no one else deserves them and no one else is able to fulfill them.

Our prayers, even though individually said, are not for us as individuals alone. That is why Jewish prayer is expressed communally in the first-person plural (even when one prays alone, he or she says "we" and rarely "I"[64]). When praying is worshipping with a community and in a liturgy formulated in that community's tradition, we presently call upon God to do for us hence-forth going into the future what God promised to do for us in the past. But God did not yet completely fulfill his promises back then. Thus our prayer for the future is our hope that God will finally bring his heavenly kingdom down here on earth. Prayer expresses an eschatological hope, which is a hope for divine justice to be finally and completely executed. This finality will only come to be in a radically transformed world, "a new heaven and a new earth" (Isaiah 66:22).

Furthermore, prayer as a communal activity is our best access to God's response to our requests.[65] That is because the historical background of these prayerful requests is the biblical narration of the history of God's covenantal relationship with the people Israel, which God promises never to nullify and to ultimately consummate. "Even when the mountains move and the hills be moved, My covenant of peace will not move away from you says the Lord who loves you" (Isaiah 54:10). Thus an individual member of the covenantal community can make a more reasonable case for God to benefit her or him when that person requests from God what will enable her or him to be a happier, more proactive participant in the communal life of the covenant. Minimally this means that this person will not be impeded in keeping the commandments that constitute covenantal life.[66] Without this covenantal background, although we can cry out for God's mercy, we have no assurance that our cry is heard or even that our cry might well be answered favorably.

The reason we may request that God keep his promises is because by promising one obligates oneself. By taking a verbally expressed oath (*shevu`ah*), promising is exercising one's autonomy. Now our human autonomy is relative insofar as our promises can be annulled by higher human authority, that is, by those who have authority over us.[67] And all the more so, the Torah invalidates any autonomous promises made by us (by invoking God's name in an oath) if that promise of ours contradicts any of God's revealed commandments, thus denying God's absolute authority, which is God's autonomy both to command his creatures and to command Godself.[68]

Nevertheless, God's autonomy is not like ours. It is absolute as evidenced by the fact that God's promises cannot be annulled because there is no higher authority that could possibly annul them.[69] This in fact strengthens our claim on God to do what God has obligated Godself to do for us unconditionally. And since God has not revealed the timetable or the map for the fulfillment of his promises to us, we may not expect God to adhere to a timetable or a map of our own.[70] We may request that God completely fulfill his promises but we have no right to insist when or where that will be done. "No eye but God's has seen what He will do [*ya`aseh*] for those who wait for Him" (Isaiah 64:3).[71]

Reminding God of what God has promised and what God has fulfilled is a descriptive covenantal exercise of God-talk. The prescriptive covenantal exercise here is reminding God to fulfill what God has prescribed to Godself by his own promises; and it is reminding God to help us fulfill what God has prescribed for us to do in response to them. And whereas in the Torah God prescribes to us humans what we are to do plus where and when that is to be done, in prayer we may only remind God of what God has prescribed to Godself but never the where and when of the fulfillment of God's covenantal promise.

On your walls, Jerusalem, I have appointed watchers, All day and all night they are never silent. Those reminding [*ha-mazkirim*] the Lord, don't be quiet, and don't be quiet to Him, until He establishes and until He makes Jerusalem praised on earth (Isaiah 62:6–7)[72]

NOTES

1. M. Tamid 7.4.

2. In fact, there were those in ancient Israel who believed that outside the land of Israel, an Israelite couldn't worship God (I Sam. 26:19; also see Jonah 2:5). This at least implies God cannot be spoken of in any language other than Hebrew as the "holy language" (*lashon ha-qodesh*) spoken in the Temple. For rabbinic nuancing of this absolute difference of kind turning it into a difference of degree, see T. Avodah Zarah 4.5 and B. Ketubot 110b re I Sam. 26:19.

3. *Ecclesiasticus* (Sirachides), prologue; *Sofrim* 1.8, ed. Higger, 101–2 a là B. Megillah 9a–b.

4. *Letter of Aristeas*; Josephus, *Antiquities,* 12.34–109; M. Megillah 1.8; Y. Megillah 1.9/71c; B. Megillah 9b re Gen. 9:27; B. Baba Kama 83a.

5. See Mal. 3:16; B. Menahot 110a re Mal. 1:11.

6. Originally this principle was expressed by Rabbi Ishmael explaining why, in prescriptive passages, the Torah sometimes uses what appears to be superfluous wordage. That is because the Torah is like ordinary human discourse, being more verbose than is actually necessary to convey its meaning (B. Sanhedrin 64b re Num. 15:31; Y. Shabbat 19.2/17a and Y. Sotah 8.1/22b re Gen. 17:13; B. Avodah Zarah 27a re Gen. 17:13 and *Tos.,* s.v. "dibbrah Torah"). See the magisterial work of Abraham Joshua Heschel, *Heavenly Torah,* trans. G. Tucker and L. Levin (New York: Continuum, 2005), passim. Also see D. Novak, "The Talmud as a Source for Philosophical Reflection" in *History of Jewish Philosophy,* ed. D. H. Frank and O. Leaman (London and New York: Routledge, 1997), 62–80. (For the notion, however, that human language is very different from biblical Language, see Y. Nedarim 6.1/39c and 8.1/40d.) This principle was much later taken by Maimonides in a very different direction (*Guide of the Perplexed,* 1.26), to explain how biblical language describing God's acts in anthropomorphic terms is a concession to the intellectual deficiency of the masses, who cannot even imagine any act whatsoever and by whomever that is not bodily action. Hence this term explains why much God-talk in the Bible must be taken by cognoscenti figuratively rather than literally. Indeed, were every statement in the Torah speaking of God's action to be read literally, the Torah would contain significant contradictions (MT: Yesodei ha-Torah, 1.8–9, very likely leading intelligent readers to conclude that the Torah is the work of an irrational author (*Guide,* 3.26 re Deut. 4:6).

7. For the notion that God spoke to the people Israel at Mount Sinai in the Egyptian language they had already been speaking so that God's word would be intelligible to them, see *Esther Rabbah,* 4.12 re Exod. 20:2, ed. Tabory-Atzmon, 95; *Pesiqta Rabbati,* chap. 21, ed. Friedmann, 106. Also see Abraham ibn Ezra's comment on Exod. 8:15 for the notion that the Egyptians were not atheists, hence God-talk was not foreign to them and could be expressed in their language.

8. Note Jacques Maritain, *Existence and the Existent,* trans. L. Galantierre and G. B. Phelan (Garden City, NY: Image Books, 1956), 21: "*Veritas sequitur esse rerum.* Truth follows upon the existence of things. . . . Truth is the adequation of the

immanence of thought with what exists outside our thought." This is based on Aristotle, *Metaphysics*, 9.10/1051b5–10, and Thomas Aquinas, *De Veritate*, art. 1.

9. See Karl Barth, *Fides Quaerens Intellectum*, trans. I. W. Robertson (London: SCM Press, 1960), 75.

10. The single human language of a truly united humankind, fully adequate to God-talk, is an eschatological desideratum (B. Avodah Zarah 24a re Zep. 3:9; *Yalqut Shimoni*: Zephaniah, no. 567.3 re Gen. 11:3).

11. For hearing (*shamo`a*) as understanding see e.g., Deut. 28:49 and Rashi's comment thereon; B. Shabbat 88a re Ps. 103:20; Maimonides, *Guide of the Perplexed*, 1.45.

12. In *Tractatus Logico-Philosophicus*, 5.6, trans. D. F. Pears and B. F. McGuiness (London: Routledge & Kegan Paul, 1961), 114–15, Wittgenstein stated, "The limits (*Grenzen*) of my language mean the limits of my world (*meiner Welt*)." Hence the famous preface and conclusion of the *Tractatus*: "What one cannot speak about, thereof (*darüber*) one must be silent" (2–3, 150–51). And he states (6.432, 148–49), "How things are in the world is a matter of complete indifference for what is higher (*das Höhere*). God does not reveal himself (*offenbart sich*) in the world." All that Wittgenstein is saying is that in "my language" (*meine Sprache*) there is no place for God to speak because God-talk has no place to be expressed therein. Nevertheless, in what Wittgenstein himself called "ordinary language" (*Umgangssprache*) in *Tractatus*, 4.002, God does speak and is spoken of in a way that is understandable to fluent speakers of that language. Cf. *Philosophical Investigations,* 2nd ed., 1.18, trans. G. E. M. Anscombe (New York: Macmillan, 1958), 8, where Wittgenstein speaks of "our language" (*unsere Sprache*). Now considering his rejection of "private languages" (ibid., 1.256–88, 90–99), *unsere Sprache* is not only the present means of public communication, it is just as much historically inherited, transmitted, and developed by speakers in the cultural-linguistic community where it has been traditionally spoken. In fact, in Ludwig Wittgenstein's own native German, as well as in his acquired English, God-talk is deeply embedded.

13. In 1994 while atheist philosopher Richard Rorty and I were colleagues in the University of Virginia, we had a well-attended debate there on whether God can be invoked in a democratic conversation or not. Rorty wrote up his argument there in an article, "Religion as Conversation-Stopper," *Common Knowledge* 3 (1994): 1–6. For my argument, see *Natural Law in Judaism* (Cambridge: Cambridge University Press, 1998), 12–26.

14. See Paul Ricoeur, "The Language of Faith" in *The Philosophy of Paul Ricoeur*, ed. C. E. Reagan and D. Stewart (Boston: Beacon Press, 1978), 231–38.

15. Still the best known and most influential philosophic dismissal of God-talk from rational discourse is found in A. J. Ayer, *Language, Truth and Logic* (New York: Dover Publications, 1952). Note: "All utterances about the nature of God are nonsensical (115). . . . The mere existence of the noun ['god'] is enough to foster the illusion that there is a real, or at least a possible entity corresponding to it (116)" For a philosophically cogent refutation of all this, see Alvin Plantinga, "Verificationism and Other Atheologica," *God and Other Minds* (Ithaca, NY: Cornell University Press, 1967), 156–83. For the countermovement against the narrowness of the logical

positivism of Ayer et al. already in the 1940s, see C. MacCamhall and R. Wiseman, *Metaphysical Animals* (New York: Doubleday, 2022).

16. See Michael Polanyi, *Personal Knowledge* (New York: Harper Torchbooks, 1962), 203–16.

17. "He made us and not [*l'o*] we ourselves." (Psalms 100:3) This translation follows the *khetiv* or unvocalized text rather than the *qerē* or vocalized Massoretic variant. See Rashi's comment thereon. Use of either text is acceptable in rabbinic biblical exegesis (see B. Sukkah 6b re Lev. 23:42–43).

18. See D. Novak, *Covenantal Rights: A Study in Jewish Political Theory* (Princeton, NJ: Princeton University Press, 2000), 36–55.

19. Along these lines, Immanuel Kant in his very theoretical *Critique of Practical Reason*, trans. W. S. Pluhar (Indianapolis: Hackett Publishing Co., 2002) writes, "But who indeed could introduce [*einführen*] a principle of all morality and, as it were, first invent morality—just as if before him the world had been in ignorance or in thoroughgoing error what [one's] duty is?" (12, n. 83).

20. B. Sanhedrin 56a–b re Gen. 2:16; MT: Melakhim, 8.11; "Letter to Joseph ibn Jabar," *Igrot ha-Rambam*, ed. Y. Shilat (Maaleh Adumim, Israel: Maaliyot Press, 1988), 1:411.

21. *The Idea of a Christian Society*, 2nd ed. (London: Faber and Faber, 1982), 82.

22. The by now classic statement of this kind of dismissal of God-talk is Freud's 1927 book, *The Future of an Illusion*, trans. W. D. Robson-Scott, ed. J. Strachey (Garden City, NY: Doubleday, 1964). Note: "It would be an undoubted advantage if we leave God out altogether and honestly admit the purely human origin of all the regulations and precepts of civilization" (67). For a critique of Freud, see D. Novak, "On Freud's Theory of Law and Religion," *International Journal of Law and Psychiatry* (2016): 48:24–34.

23. Émile Durkheim, *Elementary Form of the Religious Life*, trans. J. W. Swain (New York: Free Press, 1965), 236: "The god of the clan, the totemic principle, can therefore be nothing else than the clan itself, personified and represented to the imagination under the visible form of the animal or vegetable which serves as totem."

24. The name *elohim* (usually translated "God" or "gods") generally means authority, whether divine or human (B. Sanhedrin 66a re Exod. 22:27).

25. Aristotle, *Politics*, 1.2/1253a1–15.

26. The classic Jewish statement of the argument from design was made in the first century CE by Philo. "The first men sought to find how we came to conceive [*enoēsamen*] of the Deity . . . that it was from the world [*apo tou kosmou*] and its constituent parts and the forces subsisting in these that we gained our apprehension of the First Cause [*epoiēsametha tou aitiou*]. . . . Anyone entering this world . . . he will surely argue [*logieitai*] that these have not been wrought without consummate art [*technēs*] . . . apprehend[ing] God by means of a shadow, discerning the Artificer [*ton technitēn*] by means of His works [*dia tōn ergōn*]." *Legum Allegoria*, 2.32.97–98, *Philo*, trans. F. H. Colson and G. H. Whitaker (Cambridge, MA: Harvard University Press, 1929), 1:366–69. A possible rabbinic version of the argument from design is found in *Beresheet Rabbah* 39.1 re Gen. 12:1, and *Midrash ha-Gadol*: Genesis re Gen. 12.1, ed. Margulies, 210–11.

27. The Targumim translate "He [God] breathed into his nostrils the breath of life [*nishmat hayyim*]" (Gen. 2:7) as "humans receiving the power of speech" [*le-ruaḥ memalela*].

28. B. Berakhot 7b re Gen. 15:8; *Sifre*: Devarim, no. 313 re Deut. 32:10, ed. Finkelstein, 354–55.

29. That a prescription (an "ought") cannot be derived from a description (an "is") is a valid point most famously raised by David Hume, *A Treatise of Human Nature*, 3.1.1.

30. M. Berakhot 9.2; M. Avot 3.7 and Obadiah Bertinoro's comment thereon.

31. See for example Deut. 28:69 and 29:13–14; Ezek. 20:37.

32. Whether this is the first of the specific 613 biblical commandments or whether it is a general commandment underlying the 613, that is debated by Maimonides and Nahmanides. Maimonides holds the former view (*Sefer ha-Mitsvot*, pos. no. 1; MT; Yesodei ha-Torah, 1.6; *Guide of the Perplexed*, 2.33 re B. Makkot 23b–24a). Nahmanides holds the latter view (note on *Sefer ha-Mitsvot*, pos. no. 1). See D. Novak, *Law and Theology in Judaism* (New York: KTAV, 1974), 1:136–50.

33. M. Berakhot 2.2 re Deut. 6:4 and 11:13. Y. Berakhot 1.5/3c shows the connection of Exod. 20:2 and Deut. 6:4.

34. B. Berakhot 64a re Ps. 84:8.

35. B. Shabbat 88a–b re Prov. 11:3.

36. Judah Halevi, *Kuzari*, 1.25.

37. For the dialectic between fear of God and love of God, see Y. Sotah 5.5/20c re Deut. 6:5 and 10:20.

38. See Robert Sokolowski, *Introduction to Phenomenology* (Cambridge: Cambridge University Press, 2000), 159–61.

39. B. Berakhot 58a re I Chron. 29:11.

40. B. Baba Metsia 59b re Deut. 30:12; B. Sanhedrin 6b re II Chron. 19:6; MT: Sanhedrin 23.9.

41. For the theological necessity of this enquiry, see MT: Meilah, 8.8; *Guide of the Perplexed*, 3.26 re Deut. 4:8 and Ps. 19:10. For the best modern study of *ta`amei ha-mitsvot*, see Yizhak Heinemann, *The Reasons for the Commandments in Jewish Thought*, trans. L. Levin (Boston: Academic Studies Press, 2008).

42. B. Yoma 67b re Lev. 18:5.

43. B. Shabbat 10a re Gen. 1:3 and Exod. 18:13, and 119b re Gen. 2:1.

44. *Sifra*: Qedoshim 11.22 re Lev.20:26, ed. Weiss, 93d (also quoted in Rashi's comment on Lev. 20:26).

45. M. Sheviit 10.3; B. Gittin 36b.

46. B. Avodah Zarah 35a–36b. That the interpretation of Torah norms be reasonable, see Y. Horayot 1.1/45d re Deut. 17:11; B. Eruvin 68b; B. Pesahim 43b and Tos., s.v. "m'an;" B. Menahot 56b and Tos., s.v. "amar." Cf. *Sifre*: Devarim, no. 154 re Deut. 17:11, ed. Finkelstein, 207.

47. Maimonides's comment on M. Berakhot, end, ed. Kafih, 53.

48. M. Avot 2.1.

49. *Sifre*: Devarim, no. 49 re Deut. 11:22, ed. Finkelstein, 115; B. Shabbat 133b re Exod. 15:2 and Rashi, s.v. "hevei domeh lo"; B. Sotah 14a re Deut. 13:5; Y. Rosh

Hashanah 1.3/57a–b re Lev. 18:30 and 19:32; *Yalqut Shimoni*: Isaiah, no, 454 re Isa. 43:7; Maimonides, *Guide of the Perplexed*, 3.54 re Jer. 9:22–23.

50. Even though almost all Jewish prayers may be recited in any language (M. Sotah 7.1), after the introduction of an almost all German service in the first Reform synagogue in Hamburg in 1818, many rabbis (who later came to call themselves "Orthodox") protested vehemently. Their most prominent leader was Moses Schreiber (d. 1839), who edited and wrote the lead essay in a collection of responses *Eleh Divrei ha-Berit* (Altona, 1819). See his *Responsa Hatam Sofer*: Hoshen Mishpat, no. 192, especially his invocation of Nahmanides'scomment on Exod. 30:13 regarding the sanctity of the Hebrew as the holy language (*lashon he-qodesh*). See *Tanhuma*: Noah, no. 19; also, Meiri, *Bet ha-Behirah*: B. Berakhot 13a, ed. Dikman, 40.

51. M. Berakhot 9.3; B. Berakhot 9a re Exod. 11:2, and 34a re Num. 12:13.

52. When we experience what immediately impacts us as bad (*ra*), believing that both the good (*tov*) and the bad come from God (Isa. 45:7; Lam. 3:38), we are only required to immediately acknowledge God's inscrutable justice (M. Berakhot 9.2; B. Berakhot 60b). We are not required to immediately acknowledge God's beneficence because (in my opinion) that would be counterintuitive at this moment. Nevertheless, we are at least urged to happily acknowledge (perhaps later) that everything God causes is ultimately for our benefit (M. Berakhot 9.5 re Deut. 6:5; B. Berakhot 60b–61a; MT: Berakhot 10.3; also, B. Berakhot 5a re Prov. 3:12; B. Kiddushin 39b; MT: Teshuvah, 9.1 re Deut. 22:7).

53. B. Berakhot 9b.

54. B. Avodah Zarah 7b–8a.

55. MT: Tefillah 1.2 a là B. Berakhot 32a re Deut. 3:23–24.

56. "It came to pass after many days that the king of Egypt died, and the Israelites groaned due to their labor, they cried out, and their moaning went up to God" (Exod. 2:23). Now it does not say that they directed their cries to God but rather that their cries themselves reached God. Moses had to tell the people that God heard their cries and would redeem them (Exod. 4:28–31). Cries coming from a person's pain are spontaneous, not intending their recipient beforehand. See comment of Hayyim ibn Attar, *Or ha-Hayyim* on Exod. 2:23.

57. B. Berakhot 31a re I Sam. 1:13. On the spontaneity of prayer, see 20b.

58. B. Berakhot 21a; MT: Tefillah, 10.6.

59. B. Berakhot 33a.

60. Maimonides holds that prayer itself is a biblical commandment (*d'oraita*) that the rabbis then formulated while determining the times when the official liturgy is to be conducted (MT: Tefillah, 1.1 re B. Taanit 2a a là Deut. 11:12), Nahmanides, conversely, holds that prayer itself, and its formulations and determined times, are rabbinically, that is, humanly, instituted (*de-rabbanan*). He states this in his note on Maimonides, *Sefer ha-Mitsvot*, pos. no. 5 re B. Berakhot 20b and Rashi, s.v. "hakhi garsinan," and *Tos.*, s.v. "ba-tefillah." See Karo, *Kesef Mishnah* on MT: Tefillah, 1.1.

61. Berakhot 5.1; B. Berakhot 30b.

62. B. Ketubot 49b re Ps. 147:9; B. Kiddushin 31a.

63. Exod. 22:22 and Nahmanides's comment thereon. Cf. B. Baba Kama 93a and *Tos.*, s.v. "d'ikka."

64. Cf. B. Berakhot 17a.
65. B. Berakhot 7b–8a; MT: Tefillah, 8.1 and Karo, *Kesef Mishneh* thereon.
66. MT: Teshuvah, 9.1.
67. B. Hagigah 10a re Num. 30:3.
68. M. Shevuot 3.8.
69. B. Berakhot 32a re Exod. 32:13.
70. B. Sanhedrin 97b re Isa. 30:18.
71. B. Berakhot 34b.
72. B. Menahot 87a and Rahi, s.v. "ki."

Chapter 2

What Is Jewish Theology?

Two Views of Jewish Theology

Because the word "theology" is not part of the vocabulary of most Jews, even of most religiously learned Jews, those advocating that the enterprise of theology be acknowledged as an essential component of the Jewish tradition, and thus an enterprise to be continued, must first define the concept "theology." They must then show the indispensability of theology for the Jewish tradition's ongoing intelligent operation. So, instead of simply surveying the thought of various Jewish thinkers who could be called "theologians" because they engage in God-talk (the literal meaning of "theology"), but not employing the approach of any one of them, this chapter is an exercise of a certain kind of Jewish theology plus at least implying why it is to be preferred to the alternatives by those who take theology seriously. Doing theology rather than just looking at theology is a normative enterprise. It is the work of a participant in the ongoing Jewish tradition rather than that of a spectator outside it. Only participants in an enterprise have the right to apply its teachings normatively.[1] A spectator can say many true things *about* God-talk as it has been discussed in the history of Judaism. But only a participant can attempt to discuss the truth *of* Jewish God-talk by explaining it in the way he or she thinks best intends its truth.

The double task of defining theology, plus doing Jewish theology in a certain way, is clearly illustrated in the following incident.

A number of years ago, a group of traditional Jewish students at Cambridge University invited a prominent rabbi and talmudic scholar to speak to them. The main thrust of his talk was on the primacy of halakhah in Judaism and that Jews loyal to their tradition must learn and obey its legally formulated norms. He emphasized, however, that Jews do not need to engage in what is commonly called theology. In fact, he strongly implied theology should be avoided. During the question-and-answer period following the talk, a young woman (herself a student of philosophy) asked the speaker why he himself was so engaged in learning Jewish law and so obedient to its specific norms and why he thought all Jews should do likewise. He answered that he was so engaged in and obedient to Jewish law because it is the law God commands every Jew to learn and obey. The student then asked, "Jewish law is what God commands every Jew to learn and obey. Is that a legal proposition or is that a theological proposition?" In other words, doesn't the proposition with which the rabbi responded to the young woman's query itself state something God does, which is God's exercise of his unique right to command his human creatures, whom God has created to respond to his commandments? Even more so, this is God's exercise of his unique right to command the people whom God has chosen to respond to his commandments in a unique covenantal relationship.[2] This then is the justification (the because) of propositions prescribing what Jews ought to do. Indeed, by the rabbi's own justification of his insistence on learning and obedience to the law, doesn't the law's authority stand or fall on the truth or falsehood of that inherently theological proposition?

From this exchange, it seems that the rabbi and the student had two differing definitions of what theology is and whether theology is genuinely Jewish or not. If theology is genuinely Jewish, then it seems it should be engaged in by faithful and thoughtful Jews. If not, it should be eschewed. On the other hand, nobody could deny that halakhah is genuinely Jewish. Therefore, unlike theology, halakhah's Jewish authenticity is indisputable.[3] Indeed, as we shall see, showing how halakhah needs theology for its own integrity is probably the best way to advocate for the authenticity of Jewish theology. And as we shall also see, theology needs halakhah to give its exercise normative force.[4]

While it is likely he was unaware of it, the rabbi was assuming that theology is what Aristotle, who coined the term "theology" (*theologikē*), said it is, namely, what humans can theorize or speculate or philosophize about, namely, what humans can say (*logos*) about God (*theos*).[5] In this view, there is no higher human pursuit than to philosophize at this most exalted level. And Aristotle was followed by Maimonides (albeit by reading Arabic versions of Aristotle's works) on the naturally rational inclination imperative impelling humans to speculate about God.[6] However, the rabbi speaking to the Cambridge students seemed to regard such speculation as being peripheral, perhaps even antithetical, to authentic Judaism. No doubt this rabbi was part of a long tradition that regards any philosophical theology, even that of the great halakhist Maimonides, to be at best superficial apologetics and at worst a dangerous diversion from the centrality of halakhah in the Jewish tradition.[7] Although Maimonides and the rabbi would agree as to what theology is, they would strongly differ on the question of whether theology so defined is valuable or dangerous for faithful Jews.

Nevertheless, doesn't the rabbi's refusal to take theology seriously leave open the question as to why it is so necessary to differentiate Jewish law as commanded by God from a law commanded by human authorities? Certainly the Jewish tradition emphasizes the vital importance of this difference.[8] Could any Jew actually fulfill many of the commandments if he or she didn't have some notion of who this God is who commands every Jew to act one way and not act another way? In fact, it is generally accepted as indispensable for the proper performance of any of the positive commandments (*mitsvot ma`asiyot*) that the person performing the commandment intend (*kavvanah*) his or her action be done *because* it is God who has so commanded it be done.[9] But lest halakhah be turned into a kind of legal positivism (where it is irrelevant who made the law) or legal formalism (where the law makes itself), its formulators must constantly be aware that halakhah is the structuring of the directly revealed commandments of God (*ha-mitsvot*).[10] In other words, they must be ever cognizant of halakhah's theological foundations so that halakhah's foundation not be seen as arbitrary (contra legal positivism) and that halakhah not be seen as self-sufficient or autonomous (contra legal formalism). My late revered teacher Abraham Joshua Heschel denigrated this kind of legalism as "pan-halachic."[11] He rightly insisted that there is more to Judaism—but never less—than halakhah, of whose norms he himself was consistently observant.

So what kind of theology is capable of cogently grounding halakhah? What kind of theology better explains essential Jewish normativity? That is, what kind of Jewish theology is more coherent than the others and what kind better corresponds to the overall content of the Jewish tradition?

In the oldest translation of the Bible into any non-Hebraic language, the Greek Septuagint, the Hebrew *davar* or "word" is rendered *logos*. Thus the Hebrew "the word of the Lord" (*dvar adonai*) is sometimes translated *logos tou theou*, literally, "the word of God."[12] As such, it might be said that Jewish reflection on the meaning of God's word is what best denotes Jewish theology as a legitimate, indeed fruitful, Jewish intellectual enterprise. That is, theology is not what humans can say about God, rather, it is what God says to humans about ourselves.

Revelation per se is God's unmediated communication about, to, and with his people.[13] Moreover, revelation of God's word is only about the human condition insofar as God designates what enables humans to accept God's commandments and act according to them, which is because they speak to the human condition truthfully.[14] As Franz Rosenzweig argued early in the twentieth century, the affirmation of the centrality of the singular event of revelation is what distinguishes theology from philosophy of religion, the latter being about a universal human phenomenon that could be called religiosity.[15]

THE PRIMACY OF REVELATION

Surely revelation is absolutely central to Jewish theology as the methodological reflection thereon. Along these lines, Abraham Joshua Heschel
insightfully asserted that "the Bible is God's anthropology rather than man's
theology."[16] I can think of no better statement of the theology implied by the
Cambridge student's challenge to the rabbi. In fact, it could well be said that
Abraham Joshua Heschel was the most significant practitioner of rabbinic
theology in our time, which is the type of theology the Cambridge student's
challenge was alluding to. Let us now follow the implications of his own
statement just quoted.

Calling biblical revelation "God's anthropology" can have two meanings,
and it is important to see these two meanings separately and then how they
are connected.

First, revelation as God's anthropology means what God tells (*logos*) us
humans about ourselves. What God tells all us humans in general is that we
are made in God's image (*tselem elohim*) and thus we have the capacity for a
mutual though unequal relationship with God.[17] As such, God tells each and
every human who he or she essentially is. "Who I am" means that my unique
personal identity as a human creature depends on whom I am inextricably
related to.[18] Indeed, without that inextricable relation, I have no unique identity in the natural or created world.

What is unique about human nature? It is the capacity innate in every
human creature to participate in the divine-human relationship. Furthermore,
what God tells Israel or the Jewish people in particular about ourselves is that
God has chosen us as a people to live that relationship called a "covenant"
(*berit*) as a community and not just as individual persons.[19] As such, God
tells us Jews who we essentially are, what makes us a unique people in the
history of the world. Being chosen is a historical event. It is a choice God
made at a certain time, which was the time of the giving of the Torah at Sinai.
Unlike being the image of God, being a chosen people is not an innate or
natural property; rather, it is an acquired or received status given to the Jewish
people at Sinai. Also, since the covenant between God and Israel presupposes
a universal human capacity for a divine-human relationship, the difference
between the Jewish people and the rest of humankind is one of degree rather
than one of kind. The Jews and other humans are not two separate natural
species. That is why Gentiles can convert to Judaism and become full members of the Jewish people by conversion (*giyyur*).[20] (The election of Israel by
God is not racist.) Or Gentiles can develop their own kind of divine-human
relationship within their own traditions since Jews cannot claim a monopoly
on this relationship.[21]

Second, the revealed Torah as God's anthropology does not tell us who we are so that we might regard our nature as our possession or some property we have; instead, revelation tells us who we are, which is our innate capacity to do what God commands us to do with God as covenantal activity.[22] That is why the covenant is to be an interactive relationship not a static fact. Knowing who we are tells us that we are capable of doing what God wants us to do in and for the covenantal relationship. Being told what God wants us to do specifically teaches us exactly how that capacity or created potential is to be activated in the world. Moreover, like any potential, the capacity for a relationship with God is only truly appreciated when viewed retrospectively from the time it has already been activated in the world. The constitution of that covenantal relationship is the Torah, which is to be learned. The consequence of that learning is supposed to be our more likely keeping the content of that covenantal relationship, which is the commandments (*mitsvot*) God gives us as our ongoing task in the world. "Great is learning [*talmud*] Torah, for learning brings one to deeds [*ma'aseh*]."[23]

HALAKHAH AND AGGADAH

Revelation as the giving of the word of God to human recipients has two aspects: halakhah and aggadah. "Halakhah" literally means "law."[24] "Aggadah" literally means "narrative."[25] Aggadah tells us who God is by relating how God acts for and with the Jewish people.[26] Halakhah instructs us what God wants us to do and how to do it (*hora'ah*), ultimately, in response to what God has done, is doing, and will do for and with us.[27] As such, aggadah is descriptive; halakhah is prescriptive. Nevertheless, aggadic speculation is not imparting information about God apart from God's relationship with us; rather, it tells us of the God who has the right to require our obedience because of what God does for us and who persuades us that this is for our good in this world and beyond.[28] It addresses us as participants in the covenant, not as spectators looking at it from outside. Thus it could be said that halakhah presupposes aggadah insofar as aggadah contextualizes halakhah by situating it in the narrative of God's ongoing covenantal relationship with the people Israel. But we can only live that relationship throughout our history as God's people by living according to the concrete norms structured by halakhah. Paraphrasing Kant: aggadah without halakhah is empty; halakhah without aggadah is blind.[29]

The interconnection of halakhah and aggadah surely influenced a Jewishly literate Yale law professor, the late Robert Cover, who wrote, "No set of legal institutions or prescriptions exists apart from the narratives that locate it and give it meaning."[30] This article has become rightly famous and has been cited frequently.

Halakhah, neither generally nor specifically, is directly derived from aggadah, that is, aggadah is not applied halakhah.[31] Halakhah is not theological ethics. That is, it is not practice deduced from theory, which is what aggadah becomes when principles are abstracted from it by methodological theology and then applied practically "from the top down."[32] Rather, aggadah informs halakhah by guiding halakhah's operation in the world primarily by keeping halakhah's purposes in front of the halakhists so that they don't become narrow legalists. Nevertheless, while aggadah gives halakhah its why, it does not give halakhah its what or its how. For the determination of specific practice of the commandments, halakhists must turn to the normative experience of the covenanted communities (on the ground so to speak) for guidance. In that way, the Torah's immediate normative context is at hand rather than coming down from what seems to be a remote, heavenly perspective, one that seems to be oblivious to the immediate situation of the various Jewish communities. That is because people rely on the customary practice of their local community (*minhag*) as to what is to be done.[33] They are prone to reject what seems to have been imposed on them by theorists, but which is not rooted in the history of their particular community.[34] In case of doubt as to what the proper practice is to be, what is to be done there and then is not supposed to be deduced from theory; rather, one is told to "go out and see how [*ha'ich*] the community are conducting themselves [*noheg*] and conduct yourself accordingly."[35] (Of course, that means that the community is generally law-abiding; if not, then popular practice is to be changed, whenever possible.[36]) Therefore, it might be said that aggadah gives the commandments of the Torah their greater, more general context in the historical relationship between God and Israel while halakhah determined by local practice gives the commandments of the Torah their lesser, more specific context in the histories of the various Jewish communities. Moreover, the particular practices of the people, although having no obvious basis in scripture, nonetheless are considered to be a form of quasi-revelation.[37] So while more general aggadah helps halakhists not miss the forest for the trees, more specific halakhah helps theologians not miss the trees for the forest.

Torah is learned by rational discernment of its specific content as halakhah and of its more general meaning as aggadah. As aggadah, the Torah is more literally the word of God. It is the aural experience of hearing God address us. The Torah as halakhah is more literally the concrete thing from God, that is to say, it is the word now written down, thereby becoming a visible entity.[38] To be sure, one could say that the Torah's content itself emerged out of a dialogue between God and Moses.[39] Nevertheless, the dialogical relationship of Moses with God was sui generis.[40] Our dialogical relationship is between the text of the Torah and ourselves. It is when the Torah seems to be calling on us to understand it and explain it to others, and we respond accordingly by questioning the text before directly applying it.[41] This dialogue with the text of the Torah, though, is not primarily a private dialogue between an individual and the text; rather, it is public discourse among members of the Torah-discursive community. This discourse is conducted most immediately among ourselves here and now in the present. That is when it is conducted synchronically.[42] Moreover, this public discourse with the Torah is also conducted (less immediately to be sure) with members of the community from the past who have preceded us. That is when it is conducted diachronically. As an ancient rabbi put it, "Whoever says a tradition [*shemu`ah*] that came from the mouth of the one who first said it, the master of this tradition should be looked upon as if he were standing before [*ke-negdo*] this person."[43]

On the other hand, we can best experience the Torah as God's revealed word to us when we feel we are hearing it directly from God. This is the experience of certain specially graced individuals, but it is intermittent and totally unpredictable. It should be very much desired and hoped for by those who want to truly appreciate the Torah as God's unmediated word to us, yet having this feeling should not be a sine qua non of observance because it cannot be willed as one can will to understand the Torah and perform its commandments.[44] Nevertheless, our public interaction with the text of the Torah itself is not dialogical in the way the interaction of Moses with God was dialogical because unlike the personal relationship of Moses with God, no new content emerges from our personal relationship with God. Only out of our public dialogue with the text of the Torah does new content emerge such as innovative enactments (*taqqanot*) like the establishment of Hanukkah as a holiday to be celebrated regularly.[45] No new normative content, however, can emerge out of even a prophetic experience of the presence of God.[46] Nevertheless, new theological insights can emerge from our aggadic reflection on what God has done for us and with us.[47] In that way, theoretical-theological reflection can be more creative than practical-halakhic discourse can be.

CREATION, REVELATION, REDEMPTION

Now since tasks are done in the present looking toward the future whereas facts are discovered in the present looking back to the past, the living covenant ultimately looks forward to its total fulfillment by God's redemption (*ge'ulah*) of Israel and the rest of the world along with us. Just as the commandments of the Torah come from God and not from humans, so does the final fulfillment of the covenant come from God and not from humans. Only God, not any creature—not even special creatures like humans—is "the first and the last" (Isaiah 44:6). In this overall cosmic story, humankind in general and even Israel in particular come into the world always in between, neither at the beginning nor at the end. Thus the task of the interpreters of the Torah is to address the Torah to the present needs of the community both intellectual and practical. That gives us humans enough liberty to function as God's active junior partners in the covenant rather than being merely passive pawns in an exclusively divine drama. Nevertheless, we are not to regard ourselves as either initiating or consummating the covenant, of which the Torah is its constitution. Indeed, to regard ourselves as the initiators of the covenant (which is the position of many liberal Jewish thinkers) makes God into a kind of cosmic facilitator of an essentially human project, thus making God our junior partner rather than us God's junior partners. And to regard ourselves as the consummators of the covenant (which is the position of some messianically oriented Jewish thinkers) makes God into the remote first cause who began the world and then turned it over to humans to complete it without him as if we are God's successors.

This explication of theology as primarily "the word (*davar* or *logos*) of God" rather than as "human God-talk," the rubric set up by Franz Rosenzweig in his magnum opus *The Star of Redemption*, has been employed here (albeit somewhat differently from the way he formulated it). Rosenzweig saw the reality lived by Jews in the covenant (and hence the basic subject matter of Jewish theology) being demarcated by three irreducible events: creation, revelation, and redemption.

Creation can be seen as the source of the innate capacity for a relationship with God already given to us in the past before we become aware of it when actualizing it in the present. Creation is not a remembered past inasmuch as nobody ever experienced it just as nobody ever experienced their own birth. Thus creation is an event that transcends any power of ours to recollect it and use it as raw material, so to speak, for our own autonomous projects. Our invocation of creation only serves to give a universal background for the singular revelation of the Torah.[48] As such, it limits any presumption that this singular revelation is particularistic or parochial.[49]

Revelation can be seen as God's ever-ready gift to us through which we are able to actualize our potential for a content-filled relationship with God in the present. But we can only know that potential retrospectively, that is, after it has been actualized. But this is not self-caused actualization; it is not autonomous. Instead, the actualization of our capacity for a relationship with God can only be realized when God gives us the means proper to that end. Without doing the commanded content as revealed in the Torah, we can only accomplish what is ephemeral, which is a transient present that either sinks back into the forgotten, irretrievable past or is swallowed up and forgotten in a progressive, novel future.

Redemption can be seen as God's consummation of the covenant, which means that nobody who has not denied God will be excluded from the covenant.[50] There will be nobody nor anything outside the covenant. The sphere of the covenant and the sphere of all creation will become one by a divine redemptive act. Redemption will not be the end result of a present human projection into the foreseeable future, however. The futurity of redemption is much more radical.[51] Redemption will thus transcend even the imagined anticipation of what it could be like. It is infinitely more than anything we could infer in the present from our experience of the retrievable past.[52] Redemption is not an ideal to be realized by us. Instead, redemption will be the invasion of a future known only by God into the present. So as regards redemption, there is nothing for us to do but wait impatiently for it to arrive by our keeping the commandments that sustain us in the interim.[53] Our waiting for redemption also functions now as a limitation of the pretension that the consummation of the covenantal relationship is somehow or other in our own hands to finalize.[54]

HALAKHAH AND AGGADAH AT SINAI

The center of the Torah is the revelatory event at Sinai when the Decalogue was given to the entire people Israel. One can see the interrelation of aggadah and halakhah in a famous rabbinic midrash dealing with the question of why the Decalogue begins with the words "I am the Lord your God, who has brought you out of the land of Egypt, from out of slavery" (Exodus 20:2). Maimonides saw the first clause of this statement (*dibbur*), namely, "I am the Lord your God," to be a commandment to believe that God exists.[55] However, most other Jewish theologians follow Judah Halevi in seeing the statement to be God's telling the people Israel who God is in relation to us, namely, how God has acted for the people Israel in their very recent experience.[56] The midrash puts forth the following parable.

> A king who entered a province said to the people: may I rule over you? The people said to him, have you done us any good [*tovah*] that you should rule over us? So, what did he do? He built the city wall. . . . He said to them, now may I rule over you? They responded to him: yes, yes. So it is with God. He brought Israel out of Egypt. . . . When all Israel stood before Mount Sinai to accept the Torah, they became equally mindful of accepting God's kingship [*malkhut shamayim*] with joy [*be-simhah*].[57]

This midrash has been interpreted to mean that God has benefited the people, who then must be grateful in return by obeying his commandments.[58] However, doesn't this portray God as some sort of insecure parent (like King Lear) who indulges his children in order that they be forever beholden to him and thus obligated to gratefully obey his perpetual demands on them? However, most children resent this kind of gift because while the gift is finite, the grateful response demanded of them is infinite. In other words, what ought to be a finite, symmetrical relationship is, in fact, an asymmetrical relation benefiting the creditor and making the debtor's debt interminable. But debtors do not want a perpetual relationship with their creditor; rather, they want a finite repayment of a finite debt, which will then enable them to go their separate ways. In fact, shouldn't one try to avoid this type of dependency relationship altogether?[59] Therefore, this interpretation of the midrash does not accurately depict the covenantal relationship between God and his people with which this midrash is so concerned. Isn't the covenant an unending, asymmetrical partnership between God and his people but one that neither side wants to ever get over? God says to Israel, "My favor [*hasdi*] will not depart from you, and My covenant of peace will not move" (Isaiah 54:10).[60] And on behalf of the people Israel, Moses says to God, "If Your presence does not go [with us], do not take us up out of this [wilderness]" (Exodus 33:15). In the covenant, God is the senior partner and the Jews are the junior partners. The relationship is not meant to be terminable.

Furthermore, at the time this midrash was composed, the Jews were not experiencing God's saving beneficence to them. In fact, this midrash was composed at a time of Roman persecution of the Jewish people when God didn't seem to be vanquishing Rome for the Jewish people as God had vanquished Egypt for them.[61] Surely, seeing obedience of the commandments to be gratitude for God's salvation in this world is even more problematic today in view of recent Jewish experience of what seems to have been God's inaction during the Holocaust. So when doing theology we must be aware of the immediate historical context of the classical sources being cited. Even more so, we must be aware of the historical context in which we are now citing them and reinterpreting them for our contemporaries "where ever they might be" (Genesis 21:17). Indeed, the two historical contexts, then and now, are quite similar.

To avoid these two problems, might there be another way to interpret this midrash? What if God is not asking the people for gratitude for what God has done for them in a past event? What if, instead, God is telling the people something like this: Just as I have done good for you in the recent past events you have experienced, so will I continue to do good for you by giving you "good [*tovim*] laws and commandments" (Nehemiah 9:13). I not only have taken you out of bondage, I will teach you how to survive, even flourish, by cooperating with my beneficent rule over you, which you must accept willingly if it is to be effective in the world.[62] Moreover, whereas what God has done for the people in past events can never be taken for granted as something ready at hand but that can only be commemorated and hoped for in the future, the Torah God has given the people to learn and its commandments given to the people to do are "these words I command you this day [*ha-yom*]" (Deuteronomy 6:6). The rabbis take "this day" to mean every day, that the Torah's commandments are like a "new [*hadashah*] decree" that nobody should take as passé.[63] In other words, God is with us insofar as there is never a time when we cannot do some commandment there and then. Therefore, the initial acceptance of God's kingship is due to our being told (aggadah) how God has benefited his people in the past while the subsequent acceptance of the commandments to be obeyed can only be done properly through the halakhah informing us exactly how this obedience is to be done here and now.[64]

A woman who survived Auschwitz once told me that when her fellow prisoners taunted her for saying the *shema* each day, she said back to them, "They [the Nazis] have taken everything away from me. I won't let you take my God away from me." She was not counting on what God had done for her in the past nor was she counting on what God might do for her in the future. Instead, she was responding to what God required her to do there and then, which was to proclaim God's uniqueness even if only to herself, even if only in that hell. As a covenantal act, this involves both God and the Jewish people: the senior partner and the junior partner of the covenant.[65] Unlike many other Jewish survivors of the Holocaust, this woman did not lose her faith in the death camp. If anything her faith saved her from the kind of despair that plagued and still plagues many of those who did survive. "The righteous live through their faith [*b'emunato*]" (Habakkuk 2:4).[66] Her existential story (her aggadah) best illuminates what I think the midrash we have been discussing is teaching us. I am grateful that she trusted me enough to tell her story to me and allowed me to tell it to others.

TWO TYPES OF COMMANDMENTS AND THEIR AGGADIC COMPONENTS

Halakhah as the structuring of two different types of commandments of the Torah governing two different, though intertwined, kinds of relationships: (1) commandments that govern the God-human relationship (*bein adam le-maqom*), and (2) commandments that govern interhuman relationships (*bein adam le-havero*). In both types of commandments, aggadah as theology is needed in the attempt to discern the meaning or purpose for which the commandment was prescribed by God. Indeed, without this theological project, the commandments of the Torah would appear to be the orders of a capricious, even tyrannical, ruler.[67] This theological project is a human effort especially since the Torah itself rarely reveals the reasons of the command-ments it presents (*ta`amei ha-mitsvot*).[68] Thus aggadah not only provides the reason for the whole body of the Torah's commandments, it also provides the reasons for many of the specific commandments of the Torah.

Now no commandment pertaining to the God-human relationship is with-out some connection to interhuman relationships inasmuch as the God-human relationship is with the community in which the human members are inter-related. And no commandment pertaining to interhuman covenantal relation-ships is without some connection to the God-human relationship inasmuch as the interhuman community is an elected community whose very coming together with one another is for the sake of living the covenant with God. Nevertheless, theology functions differently in these two respective realms. In the realm of the God-human relationship, theology functions more pre-cisely as aggadah, interpreting and applying the narrative of the unique historical covenant between God and the Jewish people. In the realm of interhuman relationships, however, theology functions more philosophically, dealing ethically with natural human conditions that are not unique to the Jewish people. So for example, when it was decided that only Jews and not Gentiles ought to be required to keep the Sabbath, the reason given was that the Sabbath is what is exclusively "between Me and the children of Israel" (Exodus 31:17).[69] The reason for that seems to be that keeping the Sabbath is not a universally evident norm but that it had to be revealed to the Jewish people during their sojourn in the wilderness after leaving Egypt. Thus keeping the Sabbath is a prime example of God's unique care for his unique people. Here theology is functioning as aggadah.

On the other hand, when certain norms of the Torah pertaining to the inter-human realm could be interpreted so as to give Jews the right to take unjust advantage of Gentiles, such a right is rescinded.[70] That is because if such a right were exercised with impunity, Jewish law would seem immoral accord-ing to universal standards of morality that ought to be accepted and practiced by all humans as those created in the image of God whether they be Jews or Gentiles. The Torah is considered a further and higher specification of moral law that is universally normative and not a descent from it.[71] To interpret the law otherwise would be "desecration of God's name" (*hillul ha-shem*). Here theology is functioning philosophically. Nevertheless, even here the God-human relationship is the main factor since the rights of every human being that the Torah legislates as duties to enforce are because every human being is created in the image of God and thus deserves to have their rights as divine entitlements respected, that is, by commanding others to dutifully respond to them—minimally by not preventing their exercise, maximally by aiding their exercise.[72]

THE ENTERPRISE OF JEWISH THEOLOGY TODAY

Doing Jewish theology today requires one to employ some method of articulation taken from the surrounding world. This is not, however, the type of obsequious thinking that subordinates the Jewish tradition to something foreign to it. And this is not the type of thinking that assumes the language of the Torah is sui generis, thus requiring nothing outside itself for its explication. Instead, the need to critically employ the language of the world goes back to the rabbinic principle "The Torah speaks according to human language."[73] That is, the Torah came into a world already in place and whose inhabitants could not very well receive it, let alone interpret it, were not the Torah given in a language they had already been hearing and speaking.

Now since philosophy seems to speak worldly language with greater precision than other disciplines and since philosophy seems to deal with the deepest questions of human existence in the world, Jewish theology is, arguably, best articulated when Jewish theologians employ philosophically honed language critically.[74]

When Jewish theology is aggadah, reflecting on the experience of the covenantal relationship of the Jewish people with God, then the best philosophical method to be employed is phenomenology. By helping us perceive how we experience our personal encounter with God and enabling us to reflect on how it occurs, phenomenology is most adequate for theology's task of telling, retelling, formulating, and communicating the meaning of these irreducible experiences (what in German are called *Urphänomena*) and the truth shown therein.[75] This is especially so when dealing with the "reasons of the commandments" that pertain to the God-human relationship and how discerning these reasons helps us interpret and judge practice in this part of the Torah's domain.[76]

When Jewish theology is halakhah, prescribing how we are to actively respond to our encounters with God and our fellow humans as the praxis of revelation, the best philosophical method is that of current political philosophy. Analytic philosophers have been in the forefront of the discourse of current political philosophy, and that is why their methods should be critically employed here. Jewish interest in this type of philosophy is because of its concern with justice. Commandments pertaining to the political realm should be understood according to criteria of justice. Ultimately, they need to be justified by the justice by which God governs all creation. This is especially so when dealing with the "reasons of the commandments" that pertain to interhuman relationships and how they help us interpret and judge practice in this part of the Torah's domain.[77]

Understanding the context (via aggadah) and the content (via halakhah) of revelation has been, is, and should be the ongoing task of Jewish theology and the thinkers who engage in it. There is still much more to be done. Our task is "not to finish the work nor are we free to desist from doing it."[78] That is because "every purpose has a limit [*qets*], but Your commandment is exceedingly broad" (Psalms 119:96).[79]

NOTES

1. As philosopher Hans-Georg Gadamer wrote in *Truth and Method* (New York: Crossroad, 1982), "In both legal and theological hermeneutics there is an essential tension between the text set down . . . and the sense arrived at by its application in the particular moment of interpretation, either in judgment or in preaching . . . to be made concretely valid through being interpreted . . . according to the claim it makes" (275).

2. B. Sanhedrin 56a–b re Gen. 2:16; B. Berakhot 6a re I Chron. 17:21, Deut. 26:17 and 6:4.

3. In his 1933 essay "Was ist die jüdische Theologie?" Alexander Altmann wrote, "Every Jewish theological system that does not do justice structurally to the central position of halakhah is wrong . . . into which the factor of halakhah is built only secondarily and artificially." *The Meaning of Jewish Existence*, trans. E. Ehrlich and L. Ehrlich, ed. A. L. Ivry (Hanover, NH: Brandeis University Press, 1991), 45. In this essay, Altmann seems to be arguing against Hermann Cohen and Martin Buber. For Cohen, philosophy determines those normative aspects of the Jewish tradition to be retained by his reformed Judaism and those aspects to be eliminated from it. See his *Religion of Reason Out of the Sources of Judaism* (New York: Frederick Ungar, 1972), 1–11. For Buber, the experience of revelation trumps normativity altogether. See Martin Buber, *I and Thou*, trans. Walter Kaufmann (New York: Scribner's, 1970), 156–60. Moreover, despite being an Orthodox rabbi himself, Altmann seems to be critical of the "undoubted unpopularity in Orthodox circles of the term theology" (42). "Theology" has a very Christian connotation for Altmann, nevertheless, Altmann calls for "a theological understanding of the existence of Judaism" (42).

4. Along somewhat similar lines, see Leo Strauss, *Philosophy and Law*, trans. E. Adler (Albany: SUNY Press, 1995), 60.

5. Aristotle, *Metaphysics*, 6.1/1026a20. Since philosophy's greatest concern with Being per se (*ontos ōn*) who is God, what Aristotle calls *theologikē* is what we call "ontology." See also Maimonides, MT: Yesodei ha-Torah, 4.13; Maimonides, *Guide of the Perplexed*, 1, intro., trans. S. Pines (Chicago: University of Chicago Press, 1963), 5–11.

6. *Sefer ha-mitsvot*, pos. no. 1 and MT: Yesodei ha-Torah, 1.9 rre Exod. 20:2; *Guide*, 2.33.

7. See Gregg Stern, *Philosophy and Rabbinic Culture* (London: Routledge, 2009).

8. Note this biblical denunciation of those who do not differentiate between divine and human law: "Their fear of Me is a commandment of men [*mitsvat anashim*]. . . . The wisdom of their sages will perish" (Isa. 29:13–14).

9. M. Berakhot 2.1; B. Berakhot 13a; Joseph Karo, *Shulhan Arukh*: Orah Hayyim, 60.4; Abraham Joshua Heschel, *God in Search of Man* (New York: Farrar, Straus & Cudahy, 1955), 317–19, n. 3.

10. B. Hagigah 3b re Eccl. 12:11.

11. Heschel, *God in Search of Man*, 323. I can't begin to describe the excitement I felt when first encountering this book as a boy of fifteen. I even wrote Professor Heschel a fan letter, to which he graciously replied. It was my privilege to be his student in the Jewish Theological Seminary of America (1961–1966).

12. For example, LXX on Jer. 1:2. More often, *dvar adonai* ("the word of the Lord") is more literally translated *logos kyriou* (e.g., LXX on Jer. 1:4). See D. Novak, *Athens and Jerusalem: God, Humans, and Nature* (Toronto: University of Toronto Press, 2019), 1–19.

13. At the core of the prime revelation, viz., the revelation at Sinai, are the first two statements of the Decalogue, which the people Israel "heard directly from the mouth of God," while the rest of the Torah is mediated through Moses (B. Makkot 23b–24a re Deut. 33:4 and Exod. 20:2–3). Cf. MT: Yesodei ha-Torah, 8.1, 3; Maimonides, *Guide of the Perplexed*, 2.33 re Exod. 20:2–3 where Maimonides seems to interpret the Sinai theophany as a mass apprehension of eternal truth about God, rather than God actually speaking to the people. In fact, God's message to the people is not only mediated through Moses, it is enunciated in words by Moses (*Guide*, 1.65).

14. B. Shabbat 88b–89a re Ps. 8:1–6.

15. Franz Rosenzweig, *The Star of Redemption*, trans. B. E. Galli (Madison: University of Wisconsin Press, 2005), 151. This critical point was made by Rosenzweig in his first Jewish essay, "Atheistic Theology" (1914), trans. P. W. Franks and M. L. Morgan, *Franz Rosenzweig: Philosophical and Theological Writings* (Indianapolis, IN: Hackett, 2000), 10–24.

16. Heschel, *God in Search of Man*, 412.

17. M. Avot 3.14 re Gen. 9:6.

18. Abraham Joshua Heschel, *Who Is Man?* (Stanford, CA: Stanford University Press, 1965), 44–46.

19. M. Avot 3.14 re Deut. 14:1.

20. B. Yevamot 22a, 47a.

21. B. Sanhedrin 105a re Ps. 9:18 (the opinion of Rabbi Joshua); Meiri, *Bet ha-Behirah*: B. Avodah Zarah 20a, ed. Sofer, 46; D. Novak, *The Image of the Non-Jew in Judaism*, 2nd ed. (Portland, OR: Littman Library of Jewish Civilization, 2011).

22. Y. Rosh Hashanah 1.3/57a–b re Lev. 22:9.

23. B. Kiddushin 40b. Learning the specifics of the *mitsvot* is a halakhic exercise. Learning their more general meaning is an aggadic or theological exercise. See Maimonides's comment on M. Berakhot, end, ed. Kafih, 53, and on M. Sanhedrin, chap. 10, intro., ed. Kafih, 133. Learning Torah (whether as halakha or as aggadah) is a *mitsvah* to be done for its own sake (*li-shmah*) and not just as the means to the end of doing other more practical *mitsvot* (Maimonides, *Sefer ha-mitsvot*, pos. no.

11). Nevertheless, even learning Torah and doing other *mitsvot* for extraneous reasons is still encouraged because one could eventually come to learn and do them for their own sake (B. Nazir 23b and *Tos.,*"she-mi-tokh" re B. Berakhot 17a; Y. Hagigah 1.7/76c).

24. See Saul Lieberman, *Hellenism in Jewish Palestine*, 2nd ed. (New York: Jewish Theological Seminary of America, 1962), 83, n. 3.

25. B. Pesahim 116b re Exod. 13:8; also, B. Sotah 7b.

26. *Sifre*: Devarim, no. 49 re Deut. 11:22, ed. Finkelstein, 115.

27. *Sifra*: Shemini, ed. Weiss, 46d and B. Keritot 13a re Lev. 10:11.

28. M. Peah 1.1; M. Kiddushin 1.10.

29. Kant, *Critique of Pure Reason*, B75.

30. Robert M. Cover, "Nomos and Narrative" in *Narrative, Violence, and Law*, ed. M. Minow et al. (Ann Arbor: University of Michigan Press, 1992), 95. The rabbinic background of Cover's influential article has been explored by his Yale colleague Steven D. Fraade in "Nomos and Narrative," *Yale Journal of Law and Humanities* 17 (2005): 81–96.

31. Y. Peah 2.2/17a. See *Otsar ha-Geonim*: B. Hagigah 14a, ed. B. M. Lewin, 59–60.

32. See D. Novak, *Law and Theology in Judaism* (New York: KTAV, 1974), 1:1–6. An exception to this general principle not to deduce halakhah from theology is when Maimonides eliminates the Talmud's prescription of a blessing praising God for being "the teacher (*ha-melamed*) of Torah to His people Israel" (B. Berakhot 11b). In a little-known responsum, Maimonides argues that "whoever says this errs because God does not teach Torah to us, rather He commands us to learn it and to teach it [to ourselves]." *Teshuvot ha-Rambam*, no. 182, ed. and trans. J. Blau, 2:333. (A possible aggadic source for his halakhic opinion is B. Eruvin 54b.) Furthermore, if, as Maimonides opines in *Guide of the Perplexed*, 1.65 God didn't communicate with Moses in words, it was Moses who translated his apprehension of God's will into words and then taught them to the people (see *Midrash Tehillim*, 18.29 re Exod. 19:19 and Ps. 18:36, ed. Buber, 156). Even the pro-Maimonidean commentator Joseph Karo notes that occasionally Maimonides makes a normative judgment based on "his own (theological) opinion" (*Kesef Mishneh* on MT: Melakhim, 8.11).

33. M. Sukkah 3.11; M. Baba Metsia 7.1; M. Peah 8.2.

34. B. Avodah Zarah 35a-36a; B. Baba Batra 60b and *Tos.*, s.v. "mutav"; MT: Mamrim, 2.5–6.

35. Y. Maaser Sheni 5.2/56b; B. Berakhot 45a; also, Y. Yevamot 7.3/8a and 12.1/12c; Y. Baba Metsia 7.1/11b.

36. See B. Hullin 110a.

37. B. Pesahim 66a.

38. In Hebrew, nouns usually name the concrete products of actions named by verbs. Thus *davar* as "thing" is the concretization of the verb *dabber* as "speak." This linguistic fact has great theological significance, because the "working of creation" (*ma`aseh bere'sheet*; see B. Megillah 25a), or the "ordered creation" (*sidrei bere'sheet;* see B. Shabbat 53b) is the product of God speaking it into sustained existence. "By the word of the Lord [*bi-dvar adonai*] the heavens were made [*na`asu*]. . . . He spoke

and it came to be; He commanded and it endured [*va-ya`amod*]." (Ps. 33:6, 9). So aural revelation is often called *dibbur* by the rabbis (B. Yevamot 5b; *Vayiqra Rabbah* 1.1 re Lev. 1:1, ed. Margulies, 5–6; *Midrash ha-Gadol*: Naso 69 re Ps. 29:4, ed. Rabinowitz, 116), which is distinct from revelation written down (B. Shabbat 31a; Gittin 60b re Hos. 8:12 and Exod. 34:27). When *davar* means "word," it is often translated into Aramaic by the Targumim as *pitgama* (e.g., Deut. 17:10; Jer. 1:4); but when *davar* means "thing," it is often translated as *mid`am* (for example, Lev. 5:2; Deut. 17:1; see also B. Bekhorot 51b and Rashi, s.v. "mid`am" thereon), which is also the word used by the Targumim to translate the Hebrew *me'umah* meaning "something" into Aramaic (for example, Gen. 22:12; Deut. 13:18). The same distinction between *davar* as "word" and *davar* as "thing" appears in the Septuagint. Sometimes when *davar* clearly means spoken "word" and not tangible "thing" it is not translated into Greek as *logos* but by the more aural *rēma*, a noun coming from the verb *reō* ("flow"). See LXX on Exod. 34:27, Deut. 8:3. But when *davar* means "thing" and not spoken "word," it is sometimes translated into Greek as *pragma* ("what has been made"), a noun coming from the verb *prattō* ("make"). See LXX on Lev. 5:2; Deut. 24:1.

39. See comment of Abraham ibn Ezra on Exod. 19:19, ed. Weiser, 124.

40. Maimonides, *Guide of the Perplexed*, 2.35.

41. Y. Megillah 1.1/70a re I Chron. 28:19.

42. That is why one's participation in public Torah learning of the *bet ha-midrash* trumps private leaning at home (M. Shabbat 16.1 and Maimonides's comment thereon). In fact, Rabbi Akiva and Rabbi Hanina ben Teradyon were executed by the Romans because they violated the decree of the Roman rulers of Palestine prohibiting the public teaching of Torah (B. Berakhot 61b; B. Avodah Zarah 18a). Furthermore, this communal learning has been more exoteric for the larger community (B. Berakhot 28a; Y. Horayot 3.4/48b; B. Megillah 4a), and more esoteric for the more select community of scholars (B. Berakhot 8a; M. Hagigah 2.1).

43. Y. Shabbat 1.2/3a re Ps. 39:7. See also B. Sanhedrin 90b and Y. Berakhot 2.1/4b re Cant. 7:10. Moreover, Torah learning is often conducted by the rabbis diachronically, sometimes ignoring chronological sequence (B. Rosh Hashanah 30a–b; B. Sanhedrin 22b and 83b–84a re Ezek. 44:9; also, B. Menahot 29b). That might be because anything considered new is really something already revealed at Sinai (Y. Peah 2.4/17a re Eccl. 1:10), where it is taught the souls of all the people Israel were present (*Tanhuma*: Nitsavim, no. 3 re Deut. 29:13–14).

44. We see this in Franz Rosenzweig's famous distinction between *mitsvah* as "commandment" (*Gebot*) and halakhah as "law" (*Gesetz*). Rosenzweig doesn't think the two are antithetical as does Buber (see *supra*, n. 3), only rejecting the view of those who think the observance of Jewish law only requires the affirmation of a remote legislator rather than the ever-present One who directly commands us. This comes out in his exchange with Buber (and others like him) in *On Jewish Learning*, trans. W. Wolf, ed. N. N. Glatzer (New York: Schocken Books, 1955), 109–24. In his 1923 essay *Die Bauleute*, published posthumously in *Kleinere Schriften*, ed. Edith Rosenzweig (Berlin: Schocken Verlag, 1937), Rosenzweig wrote, "Law must become again immediate [*unmittelbar*] commandment" (116).

45. B. Shabbat 23a re Deut. 17:11.

46. Y. Megillah 1.5/70d; B. Baba Metsia 59b re Deut. 30:12.

47. Whereas a scriptural text should optimally have but one halakhic meaning (see B. Shabbat 64a and Rabbenu Hananel thereon; Y. Sanhedrin 3.9/21c re Deut. 19:17 and Num. 11:26), a scriptural text can have many aggadic meanings (*Bemidbar Rabbah* 13.15 re Amos 6:6 and Num. 15:16).

48. See D. Novak, "Creation" in *The Cambridge History of Jewish Philosophy: The Modern Era*, ed. M. Kavka, Z. Braiterman, and D. Novak (Cambridge: Cambridge University Press, 2012), 385–86.

49. Nahmanides's comment (contra Rashi) on Gen. 1:1.

50. B. Sanhedrin 105a re Ps. 9:18 (the opinion of Rabbi Joshua); MT: Melakhim, 8.11.

51. B. Sanhedrin 111b re Isa. 28:5. This radical, unforeseen future (*atid* or *l'atid la-vo*) is the frequent subject of aggadic speculation (see M. Uqtsin 3.12 re Prov. 8:21). The foreseeable future, however, is the subject of halakhic deliberation (see M. Ketubot 9.6; B. Ketubot 97a; also M. Avot 2.9 and Maimonides's comment thereon).

52. B. Berakhot 34b re Isa. 64:3.

53. Whether the *mitsvot*, practiced in the present but anticipating the radical, eschatological future, will obtain in that future or not is a question debated by the rabbis (T. Berakhot 1.10–11 re Deut. 16:3 and Jer. 23:7–8; *Vayiqra Rabbah* 13.3 re Lev. 7:24, ed. Margulies, 276–79).

54. B. Sanhedrin 97b re Isa. 30:18 and Jer. 3:14, and Rashi, s.v. "dyo" and "ba'alti" thereon.

55. *Sefer ha-Mitsvot*, pos. no. 1; MT: Yesodei ha-Torah, 1.6; Maimonides, *Guide of the Perplexed*, 2.33.

56. *Kuzari*, 1.25.

57. *Mekhilta de-Rabbi Ishmael*: Yitro 5, ed. Horovitz-Rabin, 219. See *Shemot Rabbah* 29.2 re Exod. 20:2. This seems to say that the acceptance of the Torah by the people Israel at Sinai was voluntary initially. Cf. B. Shabbat 88a–b where it says that the initial acceptance of the Torah at Sinai was compulsory and that their voluntary acceptance of the Torah came centuries later (re Est. 9:27).

58. *Mishnat Rabbi Eliezer*, chap. 7, ed. Enelow, 137–38.

59. B. Baba Batra 51a re Prov. 22:7 and 110a; MT: Mattnot Aniyyim, 10.18 re B. Pesahim 112a.

60. B. Berakhot 32a re Exod. 32:13.

61. See B. Gittin 56b re Exod. 15:11.

62. B. Shabbat 88a re Est. 9:27.

63. *Sifre*: Devarim, no. 33, ed. Finkelstein, 59.

64. M. Berakhot 2.2.

65. B. Shabbat 119b re Gen. 2:1. Cf. T. Sanhedrin 8.7 and B. Sanhedrin 38a, where it is stated that the first human (*adam ha-ri'shon*) was the last creature created by God in order to refute the claim of those who might otherwise say that "God had a partner [*shuttaf*] in the act of creation." However, in talmudic fashion, we might reconcile this seeming contradiction of saying God has a partner and God doesn't have a partner as follows: It is presumptuous to speak of humans as God's equal partners but it is not presumptuous to speak of humans imitating God as his junior partners (B. Shabbat

10a re Exod. 18:13 and Gen. 1:5). Indeed, presuming to be God's equals is how the serpent tempted the first humans to defy God (Gen. 3:5). See *Beresheet Rabbah* 19.4, ed. Theodor-Albeck, 172–73; also B. Sukkah 45b re Exod. 22:19.

66. Being faithful (*emunah*) is considered to be the one act anybody can do under any circumstances (B. Makkot 24a and Rashi, s.v. "ve-h`emidan"). See Y. Berakhot 9.5/14d re Ps. 34:8.

67. Maimonides, *Guide of the Perplexed*, 2.40; 3.26.

68. B. Sanhedrin 21a–b re Deut. 17:16–17.

69. B. Sanhedrin 58b re Gen. 8:22; *Devarim Rabbah* 1.18; *Shemot Rabbah* 25.16 re Exod. 16:29. Cf. Maimonides, *Guide of the Perplexed*, 2.31 and 3.43.

70. B. Baba Kama 113a–b re Deut. 22:3; also, Y. Sheviit 6.1/36c re Josh. 10:1; MT: Melakhim, 6.1, 4.

71. B. Yevamot 22a; B. Sanhedrin 59a.

72. B. Shabbat 31a; Y. Nedarim 9.4/41c re Gen. 5:1; M. Avot 3.14 re Gen. 9:6. See D. Novak, *Covenantal Rights* (Princeton, NJ: Princeton University Press, 2000).

73. The most profound treatment of the theological significance of this principle is Abraham Joshua Heschel, *Heavenly Torah: As Refracted through the Generations*, trans. G. Tucker and L. Levin (New York: Continuum, 2005), 47–56, 659–68.

74. The first modern Jewish thinker to designate theology as an integral Jewish discipline was Abraham Geiger. In his 1849 work *Einleitung in das Studium der jüdischen Theologie*, Geiger argued for the need of Jewish theologians to employ philosophy in their thought. See his *Nachgelassene Schriften*, ed. L. Geiger (Berlin: Louis Gerschel, 1875), 2:6–7. By 1835–1838 Geiger had founded and edited the journal *Wissenschafliche Zeitschrift für jüdische Theologie*.

75. The late Jewish philosopher Emil Fackenheim called them "root experiences" in his book *God's Presence in History* (New York: New York University Press, 1970).

76. As precedent for this kind of phenomenological reflection, see the comment of Nahmanides on Exod. 3:12.

77. As precedent for this kind of analytic reflection, see Maimonides, MT: Rotseah, 4.9; Maimonides, *Guide of the Perplexed*, 3.40.

78. M. Avot 2.21.

79. See B. Eruvin 21a and Rashi, s.v. "le-khol" thereon.

Chapter 3

The Inner Life of God

God's Thoughts

Doesn't it seem quite audacious to speak of God's thoughts, the content of God's inner life? Doesn't scripture report God declaring, "My thoughts (*mahshavotai*) are not your thoughts" (Isaiah 55:8)? Yet as we shall see, the rabbis (in the Talmud and cognate rabbinic sources) speak about God's thoughts. Yet how could they do so without any access to God's thoughts? How can any human say anything cogent about something nobody has any access to? Isn't such talk, in fact, human speculation about what has no connection to our actual experience? Isn't this kind of mind-reading engaging in unwarranted fantasy?[1] In biblical revelation, which is the only report of God's speech we have, we are told of God's acts but rarely and allusively of what God is thinking.

Nevertheless, the word for "thought"—*mahshavah*—is used in scripture to denote both human and divine thought, however different they might actually be.[2] As such, there is an analogy between God's thoughts and the thoughts of we humans. What human thought and divine thought have in common is that they are both *practically intentional*.[3] This is what makes action rational and thus essentially different from nonrational or instinctive behavior. Rational action is purposeful. An act is rational when the person doing it can give the reason why they did what they've done, that is, they can state the purpose for which the act was done. That means an active person thinks about, or deliberates on, what they're about to do, how they're to do it, and why they should do it before deciding to do it and then finally doing it. This is how our inner thinking is connected to our outer acting. Thinking unconnected to action is fantasy; acting unconnected to thought is unintentional behavior. Action pertains to one's outer life where one relates to other persons and things in the world. Thinking, though, pertains to one's inner life where one's thoughts are interrelated. Thinking is an inner dialogue.[4]

Now if we accept that humans created in the image of God are essentially rational-active beings who can be held responsible for their purposeful actions, all the more so can we assume that the God in whose image humans are created is purposeful in his actions. The difference, though, between rational human acts and rational divine acts is that humans can be summoned for interrogation as to why they did what they did. But God is not to be so summoned. Therefore, we can only speculate about what God is thinking by inferring from what has been revealed to us of God's actions in scripture and especially in God's interactions with us; that is, either what God commands us to do for him or what God does for us.[5]

Of course in order to engage in authentic theological speculation, one has to take biblical revelation at face value. This is how the Jewish people have experienced scripture as a seamless garment however the text itself might have been put together.[6] Moreover, one has to trust the biblical authors enough to believe they meant what they said and that they themselves were convinced they were truthfully reporting what God had revealed to them. (That they were neither lying nor delusional cannot be proven or disproven.) The revelation of God's deeds and God's words are the prime data to be explained. Authentic theological speculation deals with the thinking that lies behind the words and deeds of God found in the only text we have to speculate about. This speculation is a much more difficult task than even the theological exegesis of scripture.[7] Speculation concerns what is a priori, what lies behind what scripture asserts. Exegesis, though, concerns what is a posteriori, what comes after or follows from scriptural assertions.

THE METAPHYSICAL VIEW OF GOD'S
INNER AND OUTER LIFE

The inner-outer question as it pertains to God can be seen as centered on the meaning of God's response to Moses when he asks, "What is His name?" (*mah shemo*; Exodus 3:13). The answer from God is often translated "I am what I am" (*ehyeh asher ehyeh*; Exodus 3:14).[8] Moses seems to be asking what God Himself is. That is, what is God's essence? What is it without which God wouldn't be God? Without this, God wouldn't be the absolute, the one "whom nothing greater could be thought of" (*id quo maius cogitari necquit*) in the words of Anselm of Canterbury.[9] This seems to be a question about God's inner life, which is self-sufficient and thus doesn't need to engage in any external relations at all. The Septuagint, the earliest translation of the Torah into Greek and surely influenced by Greek philosophy, answers in the affirmative: "I am Being" (*eimi ho ōn*).[10] Following the Septuagint, an apocryphal work refers to God as "the Being" (*ton onta*) whom humans are naturally ignorant of.[11] Continuing this theological trajectory, the first-century Hellenistic Jewish theologian Philo takes Exodus 3:14 to mean that God alone (*monos*) is "truly the one authentic Being" (*to einai*); everything else that is not-God (namely, creation) is "non-being (*ouk ontōn*) by comparison (*kata to einai*)," that is, they are relative to Being. Nevertheless, created beings still "reflect" (*apeikonisma*) God-Being.[12] This is the what has been called *analogia entis*, implying our human being is in some ways like God's divine Being.[13] How then do created beings (*ens creatum*), especially created human beings reflect God's uncreated Being?

Maimonides sees Exodus 3:14 as declaring God to be "the necessary existent" (*ha-mehuyyav ha-metsi'ut*).[14] He takes the Tetragrammaton (YHVH) to "signify the essence (*etsem*) and true reality of God," which is God's unique name, giving God's essence a proper name.[15] Hence the Tetragrammaton is God's proper name or *who* God is, while *ehyeh asher ehyeh* tells *what* God is, namely, the Necessary Existent.[16] All created beings, though, do not necessarily exist. They only exist because God exists and has willed them to exist contingently. Thus God's necessity is both *ad intra* and *ad extra*. Internally, it means that God could not not-exist. Externally, it means that God's prior existence is necessary for subsequent existents to exist contingently. God could very well exist without there being any other existents at all. But every other existent could not exist without God's prior existence, from which God's wills them into existence.

This difference between existence and essence goes back to Aristotle's differentiation of "whether it is" (*ei esti*) and "what it is" (*ti estin*).[17] In all other beings, essence and existence are formally separate but substantially united insofar as there is no creature that simply exists without existing as some thing or other. To define a creature's essence or nature means that this particular being wouldn't be what we call it without the specific characteristics that distinguish it from beings of another species. This specific nature thus defines any being to which it pertains. So a dog wouldn't be what we call a dog without the characteristics that distinguish dogs from cats. However, no particular dog has to exist as a dog or as anything else for that matter. In fact, the whole species of dogs doesn't have to exist. While the existence of the species is necessary for a particular dog to be a dog, the existence of the species itself is not necessary. Rather, its existence is contingent on God's creative will.[18]

God's infinite existence is God's essence insofar as God-Being is not confined by any "whatness" or quiddity. Hence we can only say that God exists (*an sit*) but not what God's existence essentially consists of (*quid est*). Indeed, to say what God's inner life consists of would put God into a finite category, which couldn't possibly contain the one who is infinite or limitless and, therefore, no boundaries could contain him. God is a category in and of itself having but one member.[19] Hence the category and its one member are identical. That is why God is unique (*ehad*). That identity would only be belied were the category to contain more than one member. "The Lord He is God; the Lord He is God!" (I Kings 18:39).[20] Along these lines, a French philosopher is reported to have quipped, "*Un Dieu defini, c'est un Dieu fini.*"

In one very significant way, God-as-Being taught by the Septuagint is not like God-as-Being taught by Aristotle. For Aristotle, God's Being is not only God's self-sufficiency but also God's total indifference to any relationship at all.[21] God has no "other." Conversely, scripture teaches us God is "the Creator" (*ha*-borē) who intends "others," namely, created beings. Now in this Hellenistic Jewish theology, God's creating is an act of gracious or generous will for these others. But it is not a reaction to anything creatures have done for or against God. God has no interaction with what is not-God. The relation is all one-way. God's action is transitive but not transactional. (For Aristotle, though, God's action is wholly intransitive, solely reflexive, and certainly not transactional.) Therefore, God's self-sufficiency, God's total independence extends to God's transitive action to be the wholly sufficient cause of all dependent beings. In other words, God *effects* creation but is not *affected by* creation. God's inwardness is in no way affected by God's outwardness.

This divine necessity for creatures to exist because of God's creativity is beautifully expressed by the poet-theologian T. S. Eliot: "Those who deny Thee could not deny, if Thou didst not exist; / and their denial is never complete, / for if it were so, they would not exist."[22] Moreover, to deny the necessary existence of God is to presume that all that exists exists accidentally rather than contingently. That presumes, though, that nothing exists intentionally.

However, on what basis can we cogently assume that our existence is contingent on God's intentions? Do we infer the necessary existence of God from the orderly existence of finite beings? Or, do we know God's necessary existence only when God presents Godself to us, when we are addressed by God in an unprecedented revelatory event, an event that shows the contingency of those for whom the event was meant?

KABBALAH: TOTAL DIVINE INWARDNESS

The metaphysical notion of God as Being is also developed in Kabbalah. Although the kabbalists strongly differed with the more explicitly philosophical metaphysics of those Jewish thinkers who were admittedly influenced by Aristotelian ontology (as was the Septuagint), they were engaging in metaphysical speculation nonetheless.

In Kabbalah, there is no relation between the inner and the outer in the life of God because there is no divine exteriority. There is only divine interiority that includes all reality. There being nothing outside God, there is nothing for God to relate Godself to. All reality is essentially divine. Anything outside God is considered demonic nonbeing (*sitra aḥra*, literally, "the other side").[23] As such, the inwardness of God contains all reality as parts of the divine whole even though the infinite whole (*ein sof*, literally, "without end") is greater than the sum of its finite parts (*sefirot*, literally, "spheres"), which are ten in number.[24] This doesn't mean that God as infinite Being is coextensive with God's manifestations in the *sefirot*. It is only in the realm of the *sefirot*, though, that we humans can relate to the divine. It is this realm where we can speak to God as "You" (*attah*). Conversely, when speaking about God transcending his finite manifestations, we can only allude to God as "He" (*hu*) who is totally concealed (*satim*), concealed from everything finite.[25] Some philosophers have called this view "pan-en-theism," namely, "everything is in God," which is essentially different from the pantheistic claim that "God is everything."[26]

The kabbalists are not the only proponents of panentheism, despite their claim that Kabbalah is divine revelation and not human thought (not even human thought about divine revelation of the Torah).[27] Like their rationalist adversaries, the kabbalists too were influenced by an older philosophical tradition even though they hardly ever admitted it. Moreover, even though it is most unlikely the kabbalists knew of the Septuagint's equation of God and Being, they are certainly in the Septuagint's camp nonetheless.[28] Moreover, they go farther toward a monistic metaphysics than do the authors of the Septuagint. The authors of the Septuagint and the Greek philosophers who influenced them could say that "God is Being" (*to ōn*) and everything else is "beings" (*ta onta*), and the two are distinct.[29] For the kabbalists, though, God is Being and everything else doesn't exist at all even in a more diminished state. Everything outside of God is no-being at all.

All of this comes out in the treatment of Exodus 3:14 in the *Zohar*, the foundational kabbalistic text. There it states, "Mystery of the matter is as follows, **Ehyeh**, *I am*—totality of all . . . hidden and not revealed. Once a beginning [*sheiruta*] emerges . . . to channel all, then it is called **asher ehyeh**, *that I am*."[30] Now this is not an outward process moving from God to not-God, from creator to creation. Instead, it is a process of eternal emanation within the Godhead itself.[31]

However, since everything is in God and the covenanted people are the most immediate conscious participants in the divine life, how can their observance of the commandments be understood in this panentheistic view? Don't all the commandments coming from God presuppose a world that is not-God where they are to be kept? The acts commanded by God are not divine acts but human acts, nor is the place where they are to be kept the inner life of God.[32] As the rabbis put it, "The Torah is not in heaven."[33] Nevertheless, the kabbalists do not accept this separation of God and the created world. For them, the commandments of the Torah are actually interactions within the divine itself (*elohut*). Thus acts commanded by God to humans in the Torah are actually symbolic participations in God's all-inclusivity. Even though the commanded acts look mundane or worldly prima facie, their true reality is divine.[34]

Now all of this saves Kabbalah from the charge that it weakens the commitment of Jews to the specific details of the commandments (*diqduqei mitsvot*), which are themselves quite worldly, by making the reality of the commandments so unworldly. In fact, because of its rich, attractive symbolism, Kabbalah has captured the imagination and practical loyalty of many law-abiding Jews even today.[35] Thus Kabbalah has enhanced their observance of the commandments by giving many seemingly mundane acts such cosmic significance that can be spoken of. As such, the problem with Kabbalah (which is hardly mine alone) is with its ontology and not with its sincere commitment to normative Jewish praxis.

It could be charged that the kabbalists say too much about God's inwardness. This leads us to question its monotheism because of its assertion of inner divine multiplicity. In fact, when Kabbalah first became widely known in the late twelfth century, its theological critics were quick to question it on this very point.[36] The background of this critique is important to understand since it has affected Jewish theology ever since.

Already as early as the ninth century, with the rise of Islam and the transmission of Greek philosophy through Arabic translations, Muslim theologians were criticizing Judaism for its insufficient monotheism. Their criticism centered on biblical anthropomorphism, which they held strongly implied multiplicity in God. Their criticism was philosophical in the sense that the *Quran*'s doctrine of God could be justified by the Aristotelian notion of God's transcendence of worldly involvement, whereas the Bible in this respect doesn't pass muster. Biblical anthropomorphisms imply God has a physical body, hence ontological multiplicity is inherent in God because anything material is divisible into multiple parts.[37]

The counterstrategy of philosophically inclined Jewish theologians was to interpret biblical anthropomorphisms figuratively as metaphors for the faithful masses, who are incapable of thinking of an incorporeal God. They can only imagine a God who is different from them in degree but not in kind, both being in their eyes corporeal. Because of the Christian doctrine of the Trinity, Christians were charged with the same insufficient monotheism by the Muslims. Hence both Jews and Christians were charged by Muslims with teaching a paradoxical monotheism: one God having many aspects or attributes. Perhaps sensing a greater philosophical affinity with Islam than with Christianity, philosophically inclined Jewish theologians joined with Muslims in making anti-trinitarian arguments.

It is certainly understandable that when Kabbalah became public in the thirteenth century in Christian Northern Spain, philosophically astute Jewish theologians were quite upset. Like Christianity, the kabbalistic doctrine of the one infinite God having ten aspects or attributes (*sefirot*) seems to be as paradoxical as the Christian doctrine of what is called the "triune God." In fact, the fourteenth-century halakhist and theologian Isaac bar Sheshet Parfat quoted an unnamed Jewish philosopher (*min ha-mitpalsim*) as quipping that the Christian "trinitarians" (*ma'aminei ha-shilush*) at least got divine multiplicity down to three aspects whereas the kabbalists elevated it to ten. Although Parfat said he was convinced of the orthodoxy (or "orthopraxis") of the kabbalists, it is clear that he was uncomfortable with their theology.[38] He furthermore claimed that his teacher Nissim of Gerona (Ran) thought that the great kabbalist Nahmanides, the teacher of his teacher Solomon ibn Adret (Rashba) had overdone his enthusiasm for Kabbalah. This shows that anti-Kabbalah was already three generations old in the very region in which it first appeared.

The type of inner divine multiplicity taught in the rabbinic tradition, however, escapes the critique of biblical anthropomorphism leveled against Judaism by Muslim theologians using philosophical weapons. Their critique was of the ontological multiplicity they saw underlying biblical anthropomorphism. Nevertheless, to speak of God deliberating in his mind between the ideas of justice and mercy (as we shall soon see) is only to speak of psychological multiplicity. Even philosophical theologians like Saadiah and Maimonides had to admit God could have multiple thoughts without assuming God has inner multiplicity. In the same way, God's multiple actions do not require us to assume that God accomplishes these actions with multiple bodily organs.[39] Whatever is physically attributed to God is, in fact, not a part of a divine whole but rather a created instrument used by God. Conversely, though, the kabbalists' doctrine of inner divine multiplicity is much more than psychological. It is, to be sure, truly metaphysical having a logic of its own. All that notwithstanding, the kabbalists cannot escape the charge that they have in fact compromised monotheistic theology not only by asserting divine multiplicity but by actually delineating it.

Looking upon the inner multiplicity of the divine life as substantial led the kabbalists to name the *sefirot* with nouns like "wisdom" (*h̲okhmah*).[40] This is different from looking upon the inner multiplicity of the divine life as functional. So saying a person is wise does not mean that this person is instantiating a divine state or attribute called "wisdom." Instead, one who is wise is acting wisely. Thus *h̲okhmah* functions adverbially, modifying a verb stating what God *does* rather than a noun stating what God *is*. God's attributes (*middot*) are capacities for action and not objects of contemplation, as we have seen earlier. "How manifold are your works O Lord. You made all of them wisely [be-*ḥokhmah asita*]" (Psalms 104:24). So when we appreciate how wisely God acts, we can then infer retrospectively that God has the capacity for such wise action

Furthermore, because everything is contained by the divine, the kabbalists had to demote the classical Jewish doctrine of *creatio ex nihilo*. Since there is multiplicity in the divine, in order to avoid the charge of this being divine pluralism (or absolute polytheism), the kabbalists taught there is an ontological hierarchy in the divine. Even though *Ein Sof* transcends the ten *sefirot*, being infinitely more than the sum of all of them, yet they are all subordinate to *Ein Sof*. Hence divine action proceeds from the top downward to the lowest *sefirah*. This eternal process is what the Neoplatonic philosophers called "emanation."[41] The kabbalists called it *atsilut*.[42] However, without this hierarchy, unified divine action would have to be seen as the result of a consensus among equals rather than the univocal action of the one and only God. As a kabbalist told Isaac bar Sheshet Parfat, the One God acts through (*b'ezeh derekh*) the subordinate *sefirot*.[43] The *sefirot* in no way function independently of *Ein Sof*, neither separately as individual deities nor even collectively in unison.

In later Kabbalah, creation is an inner divine process of "self-contraction" (*tsimtsum*), whereby the infinite God as it were makes room for multiplicity, but all this is *within* the divine life itself.[44] One could say that *tsimtsum* is what makes *atsilut* possible as a kind of inner divine a priori.[45] Nevertheless, there is still no absolute difference between God and not-God, between creator and creation, which is clearly what the doctrine of *creatio ex nihilo* teaches.[46] That is why creation (*beri'ah*) plays a far less important role in Kabbalah than it does in both rabbinic theology and in Jewish philosophical theology.[47]

However, despite their seeming demotion of creation, the kabbalists still did not deny this doctrine altogether as did Spinoza.[48] Their careful avoidance of such denial kept the kabbalists within the boundaries of Jewish tradition, within the community to whom this tradition was transmitted and who are ever transmitting it anew. Unlike Spinoza, they clearly chose to actively remain there. Indeed, the kabbalists considered themselves to be the elite of this normative community.

HERMANN COHEN: BEING AND BECOMING

The most important modern thinker in the Septuagint's camp is the German-Jewish philosopher Hermann Cohen (d. 1918). Like the Septuagint, Cohen tells us what God is. God is unqualified, absolute Being (*Sein*). By his acceptance of the Septuagint's rendition of God-as-Being, Cohen was quite explicit in acknowledging the original location of this idea to be in the thought of the pre-Socratic philosophers known as the Eleatics.[49]

In Cohen's critical reworking of the Eleatic notion of God-as-Being, God is now seen in a necessary correlation with everything that is not-God, which is qualified or relative being, now called "Becoming" (*Werden*). Cohen writes that "correlation is the most basic form of scientific thinking, of judgment in our terminology."[50] For Cohen, Being cannot even be affirmed apart from its correlation with Becoming, just as Becoming cannot be affirmed apart from its correlation with Being.[51] This correlation is dialectical rather than interrelational. All we can say of Being is that it is not-Becoming. All we can say of Becoming is that it is not-Being and will never really (*wirklich*) merge into Being. The two will ever remain in dialectical tension vis-à-vis one another. As Cohen put it with typical succinct clarity, "the uniqueness (*Einzigkeit*) of God is therefore in opposition (*entgegengesetzt*) to the universe."[52] Cohen conceives of Being as "Origin" (*Ursprung*) and Becoming as "Consequence."[53] His admitted use of logical terms is significant insofar as logic deals with necessary connections. Hence an origin is not free to do anything other than creating or generating its consequents, anymore than a premise can choose whether or not to generate a conclusion.

Nevertheless, if Being denotes God's inwardness and Becoming denotes the exteriority of the outer world, this correlation doesn't explain how God can freely choose to move from his inwardness to relations with external creation. For Cohen, Being and Becoming are necessarily correlated; neither of them can transcend the other. Yet this surely clashes with classical biblical-rabbinic theology in which God can and does transcend his creation, while his creation cannot transcend God. The relationship between God and humans is not a correlation as it is asymmetrical. God has a life apart from his creatures whereas creatures have no real life apart from God however much they might delude themselves that such ontological apartness from God is even possible. Now the God necessarily correlated with creation would not have the freedom to create or not create, nor would God have the freedom to choose or not choose his covenanted people, nor would he have the freedom to reveal his Torah or conceal it from us humans. Moreover, these choices, like all choices, are made in time. But for Cohen, Eternal Being is essentially non-temporal and thus cannot enter into the created temporal world.

Neither Being nor Becoming applies to the God-human relationship. Contra Cohen, God's *being-by-Godself* is too unknown, too transcendent, to even be correlated with human *becoming-in-the-world*. Humans, however, can only aspire to be like God in ways that God has freely revealed to them. This is what God told Moses when Moses said to God: "Do show me Yourself [*kvodekha*]" (Exodus 33:18).[54] And God's immediate answer was "No human can see Me and live" (Exodus 33:19). That is then followed by the revelation of God's imitable beneficent acts in the world (Exodus 33:19–23).[55] Indeed, God's beneficent acts performed for humans are only known because they have been revealed in the Torah, and we are commanded by the Torah to imitate them.[56] We can only love our neighbors by imitating the love God by which God has loved his people in our history.[57]

As for human "becoming," that is not the Torah's modus operandi for the covenanted people. With deference to Cohen, human action is not an unending striving for an unrealizable ethical ideal involving unending active human striving. Cohen writes of "the ethical ideal having no adequate realization (*Wirklichkeit*)," that is, in any possible world.[58] As such, humans are ever progressing through history infinitely, that is, without end.

Certainly it is more theologically cogent to say that God, not humans, will bring about the end of history, that is, when God freely chooses to do so at "the end of days" (*ahareet ha-yamim*) in "the world-yet-to-come" (*olam ha-ba*).[59] It will be God's "becoming (*ve-hayah*) the unique (*ehad*) King over all the earth" (Zechariah 14:9). That means God and God alone will definitely realize what God's unique ideal is in the unforeseeable future, which "no eye but God's has yet seen" (Isaiah 64:3).[60] Only then "will the kingdom be the Lord's" (Obadiah 1:21).[61] Yet it is a great human temptation to think we ourselves can realize this ideal end and an equally great temptation to think that the ideal end will never come about or even that God has lost interest in ever bringing it about.[62] Despite these understandable temptations, in the meantime, the covenanted people must strive through their keeping of the Torah's commandments to acknowledge God's kingship here and now and to prepare a place in the world where God's final redemption (*ge'ulah shlemah*) will be truly welcome because it has been faithfully awaited.[63]

THE EXISTENTIAL VIEW OF GOD'S INNER AND OUTER LIFE

A very different approach to Exodus 3:14 is provided by Martin Buber (d. 1965) and Franz Rosenzweig (d. 1929). Their interpretation (like any insightful translation) of this text goes back to rabbinic texts, yet they have given it a powerful modern reinterpretation. Buber and Rosenzweig translate *ehyeh asher ehyeh as* "I shall be there as the I-who-shall-be-there" (*ich werde das-ein als der ich dasein werde*).[64]

Now this use of the German word *dasein*, meaning "being-there," making it into a participle, is a most significant innovation.[65] *Dasein* is a noun that names a substance called "existence." Thus "the existence of God" is called *Dasein Gottes*. In changing the noun *Dasein* to the participle *da-sein*, Buber and Rosenzweig are following Kant who argues that "existence" does not name a substance. Instead, *Dasein* designates a relation (what Kant calls a "copula") not a substance.[66] Buber and Rosenzweig turn this into a relation *between* subjects where each is different from—*other than*—the other. In their view, *dasein* not only signifies a relation, it signifies an external relation. The two parties to the relation are outside each other. Unlike an internal relation, one is not contained in the other. Also, this is not like a part that is contained or subsumed in a larger inclusive whole nor is it like a larger whole containing both parties (and more than those two). In this regard, Kant writes, "the consciousness of my own existence (*eigenen Dasein*) is simultaneously (*zugleich*) an unmediated consciousness (*unmittelbar Bewusstsein*) of the existence of other things outside me."[67]

Following Buber's and Rosenzweig's interpretation, we could say that when God declares his *dasein* to Moses, God is saying that he has *located* Moses where God *is-there-for-and-with* Moses. That is a preview of what God's relationship will be for and with the people Israel. By saying "here I am" (*hinneni*) in response to God's calling out his name (Exodus 3:4), Moses is saying "I am here for You now." God's *being-there*, which is God's promise to be with Moses and the people Israel in the future (as God had been with the patriarchs in the past), is met by Moses's *being-here* in the present to now carry out his acceptance of God's invitation to be proactive in their relationship. Moses responds to God's having located him by answering that he is ready to do what God asks him to do in return.[68] This makes their relationship mutual but always asymmetrical nonetheless. It is not a partnership of equals.[69] "The Holy One says: to whom would you compare Me; with whom am I equal (*v'eshveh*)?" (Isaiah 40:25). The covenantal relationship is like that between teacher and pupil where the teacher always has priority over the pupil.[70]

Buber and Rosenzweig interpreted Exodus 3:14 as a statement of God's outer life, God's exteriority. Two verses earlier (Exodus 3:12), God says, "I shall be with you" (*ehyeh imakh*). This clearly speaks of God's external relationships, specifically God's covenantal relationship with the people Israel. Thus their interpretive translation seems to be a better explanation of the dialogue between God and Moses in this chapter in Exodus. It has much precedence in the Jewish tradition. Let us now look at the text closely.

Ehyeh asher ehyeh is given as God's answer to the people's question in
3:13 "What is His name" (*mah shemo*)? Some modern biblical scholars have
pointed that in the ancient Near East, knowing a god's name gave one the
power to conjure up that god.[71] That is why it was kept secret from all but
initiates in an esoteric cult lest that name be used inappropriately.[72] Knowing
a god's name gave one the power not only to locate a god but to force that
god to be present and to do the bidding of the conjurer. Along these lines,
note that the Hebrew word for "name" (*shem*) is spelled with the same three
consonants as the Hebrew word for "there" (*sham*).[73] So asking for God's
name might be like asking for God's address: where-and-when God can be
located by us, and where God must be there to be found by those who know
how to position God in our world. An address is the place where a person can
be addressed, that is, spoken-to.[74]

God's answer to this question is we humans can't locate God; we can't situ-
ate God in our world. Instead, God locates us wherever and whenever we are
to be found.[75] As a midrash puts it, "God is the place [*meqom*] of His world;
His world is not His place."[76] Therefore, since God is not to be found in our
world, the attempt to prove God's existence by locating even traces of God's
presence in ordinary experience is doubtful if not futile.[77] Thus "seek the Lord
when and where He might be found (*be-himats'o*; Isaiah 55:6)" seems to be
saying that God is only found when and where God chooses to be found,
strongly implying that God is no inert object without the choice to absent or
remove itself from being found.[78] Therefore, no name of God denotes God's
essence, which is saying *what* God is—that is, what God is necessarily—
even if all that can be said *of* God is that "God is Being itself."[79] In Exodus
3:14, God seems to be saying "I will be whoever, whenever, wherever I
choose to be."[80]

Franz Rosenzweig most definitely and explicitly takes *ehyeh asher ehyeh*
("I shall be there as the I-who-shall-be-there") not to be God's speaking
about Godself. Instead, God is speaking here of his exteriority, namely,
God's relationship with the people Israel. As the most important influence
on Rosenzweig, the eleventh-century, Spanish-Jewish theologian Judah
Halevi noted,

And God began His address to the multitude of the children of Israel . . . [say-
ing] "I am [the] God, whom you worship, who brought you out of the land of
Egypt . . ." He did not say, "I am the Creator of the world and your Creator." . . .
[This] is fitting for the whole of Israel, who knew these things, first from personal experience, and afterwards *through uninterrupted* tradition, which is equal
to the former.[81]

Now what is the difference between creation and the Exodus? Only the Exodus was experienced by the people, not only as what God did for them but even more so what God did with them.[82] The people not only remember and tell what God did for them in the past, they regularly celebrate it with God in the present.[83] From this celebratory re-experience, they even anticipate what God might do for them and with them in the future. On the other hand, though, creation is not experienced by anybody as there was nobody yet in the world to experience—being created. No one can experience being changed from nonexistence to existence—which is *creatio ex nihilo*—any more than one can experience his or her own birth. A person's creation is his or her being transformed from no place to someplace in the world. As such, it cannot be reenacted. The Exodus, conversely, was the people Israel being changed from one place to another place in the world already there, where one can experience what has occurred therein. For Halevi (with much support in scripture), the people Israel can only affirm the God whose mighty acts in the world they have experienced in the past at certain places, then celebrate them in the present anywhere, and from which they can anticipate the future redemption promised by God to them and to all humankind along with them.[84]

Only after the experience of the Exodus-event (leading up to the experience of the event of revelation at Sinai) could the people understand that the Creator-God alone is powerful enough and wise enough to be able to redeem them from being slaves to the strongest and most intelligent nation on earth, and for them never to return there and never to perish in their new liberty.[85] Thus the Exodus presupposes Creation insofar as Creation is what made the world a place where the Exodus as a unique event could possibly occur, that is, where humans could experience it. However, Creation does not entail the Exodus insofar as God's action on the world does not require God to act in the world let alone act through unique revelatory events that can be experienced by its human inhabitants. Indeed, Creation as God's acting *on* the world does not require God to act *in* the world at all.

Writing after Franz Rosenzweig's premature death, Martin Buber criticized the attempt by Jewish theologians like Philo, Saadiah, and Maimonides to turn this statement by God about Godself from a statement of God's exteriority into a statement of God's inwardness.[86] Elsewhere, Buber noted Rosenzweig's rather sarcastic remark that the despairing Hebrew slaves in Egypt hardly needed to hear a lecture on God's necessary existence. What they needed was to be assured of God's-being-with-them (*bei-ihnen-Seins*). As God is there with (*dasein*) Moses, so will God be with them.[87]

Buber refers to the paraphrase of *ehyeh asher ehyeh* by the third-century Palestinian sage Rabbi Isaac, namely, "God said to Moses to tell them (Israel) I was, I am now, and I will be the One to come in the future."[88] Rabbi Isaac goes on to say, "God said to Moses to tell them that I am with you in this oppression, and in any other oppression they will be going into, I shall be with them." (One could say, in the German terminology used by Buber and Rosenzweig, that this is a statement of God's *mitsein*, not God's *Sein*.) Buber also agrees with Rosenzweig that the idea of God's being-with-us was best developed by Judah Halevi.

Now there is a debate in the Talmud as to where God's presence (*shekhinah*) is to be found.[89] In the view of Rabbi Akiva, the *shekhinah* is regularly (*tadira*) located in the western part of the Temple, in the direction toward which the people pray there. Conversely, in Rabbi Ishmael's view, the *shekhinah* is "everywhere" (*be-khol maqom*). The problem with Rabbi Akiva's view is that it implies God is necessarily in one place as distinct from all other places, thereby limiting God's presence to someplace in the world. The problem with Rabbi Ishmael's view is that it implies that God is present everywhere in the world, implying that God wouldn't—or even couldn't—absent Godself from the world.

However, *kol maqom* might not mean "everywhere" but rather "anywhere" God desires to be present at or absent from.[90] This would remove the implication of Rabbi Akiva's view that God is necessarily "here" and not "there." That is, God is free to be present at or absent from anywhere or anytime God so chooses. Thus the freedom to be whenever or wherever God wants to be or not to be precludes the necessity of God's having to be either somewhere or everywhere. Indeed, the statement that "no place is empty of God's Presence"—as an answer to the question of why God first appeared to Moses in a lowly bush (Exodus 3:2)—might well be translated as "from no place (in the world) *could* God *not* absent Godself."[91] This is quite different from the usual interpretation of this dictum that "God is everywhere."[92] Instead, "at times God is seen and at times God is not seen. . . . At times God is to be found and at times God is not to be found."[93]

Rosenzweig deals with the inner life of God more extensively in his masterwork *The Star of Redemption*. For Rosenzweig, before creation God is self-sufficient, unrelated to anything outside Godself. God's choice to relate to the world is God's choice to move "beyond" (Rosenzweig's brilliant take on the Greek preposition *meta* in *metaphysics*) self-sufficiency or essential Being or "nature" (his take on the Greek noun *physis* or "nature" in *metaphysics*) to become involved with the world.[94] In so doing, the world is made dependent by God's choice to freely create it, thus calling the world into its radically contingent existence. Furthermore, God's mysterious inwardness is not exhausted by God's exteriority, namely, by God's freely chosen involvement with the world, which becomes God's transactions with humans via revelation.[95]

However, Rosenzweig does not speculate on what it is that is going on in the mind of God when God chooses to create the world let alone when God chooses to respond to human actions in the world. In other words, Rosenzweig is right about God's self-sufficiency. Having no essential connection to the world, God's self-sufficiency can only be alluded to; we humans cannot even imagine what God is doing in matters that have no connection to our world. The most one can do is to affirm the contingency of the world not by stating how God created the world but rather by arguing *via negativa* against anyone who states that the world is self-sufficient.[96]

All this notwithstanding, no one can positively affirm that the world is contingent on God without at least speculating how God is related to the world and how the world is related to God. This seems to involve speculating on what God might be thinking of in God's intelligent preparation for interaction with humans and what humans should be thinking of in their intelligent preparation for their interaction with God. All this involves a theory of mutuality in the divine-human relationship even though this mutuality is not symmetrical. This speculation is highly imaginative to be sure, but its continual reference to what has actually been revealed to us in scripture keeps this imaginative speculation from becoming the kind of wild fantasy that is an escape from reality rather than an attempt to fathom what lies behind it. That is to fathom what is implicit in what has been explicitly revealed.

GOD'S PRAYER

We have now at long last reached the point where we can deal with what might be a more theologically adequate way of connecting God's inwardness with God's exteriority. So let us look at a Talmud text that very much deals with our question here but one that needs considerable unpacking.

> Rabbi Yohanan in the name of Rabbi Yose: Where does Scripture inform us that God prays [*mitpalel*]? It is said, "I shall bring them to My holy mountain and make them rejoice in My house-of-prayer [*be-vet tefilati*]." (Isaiah 56:7) Now it doesn't say "their prayer" [*tefillatam*]; it says "My prayer" [*tefilati*]. From here we learn that God prays. So, what does God pray? Rav Zutra bar Toviah said in the name of Rav [that God says] "May it be My will [*yehi ratson*] that My mercy [*rahami*] will overcome My anger [*ka'asi*], and that My mercy will surge so that I will judge their [Israel's] case above and beyond the strict letter of the law [*lifnim mi-shurat ha-din*].[97]

First of all, we see this striking midrash on the passage from Isaiah, turning the possessive pronoun "My," which in the biblical text itself pertains to "house-of-prayer," and making it apply just to prayer itself. That is needed because the text itself (and no other biblical text to my knowledge) does not indicate that God prays; instead, it teaches that not only Israel but all the nations of the world pray. Prayer is an ubiquitous human practice. In pre-messianic times, though, each nation prays on its own.[98] Not until the final redemption will all the nations of the world come up to Jerusalem to pray to the Lord God along with Israel. The text speaks of what God will do for the nations of the world, not what God does by Godself. What God does by Godself can only be speculated on by astute theologians like Rabbi Yose. That speculation is deeper than ordinary exegesis.

The assertion that God prays is a novel interpretation of the verb "pray" (*mitpalel*). Indeed, the verb has to be reinterpreted this way so as to answer the charge that prayer is only a transitive human act.

Humans pray *to* God. The subject is clearly distinct from the object. God does not pray to humans nor does God pray to Godself. So far, prayer (*tefillah*) is taken to be either "beseeching" (*baqashah* in Hebrew) or "acknowledgment" (*hoda'ah* in Hebrew).[99] In either case, though, we have what Martin Buber famously called an "I-Thou" (*ich und du*) relationship between God and humans.

Rabbi Yose, however, is building his speculation regarding God's prayer to Godself on the grammar of the Hebrew text. The verb is in the *hitpa'el* form, which would normally intensify the verb *palel*, thus meaning that prayer is intensely beseeching God or that prayer is intensely praising God. Here the verb is describing transitive action. Nevertheless, the *hitpa'el* form can also make the verb it modifies reflexive or intransitive. Yet doesn't beseeching oneself imply a schizoid personality, and doesn't praising oneself imply a narcissistic personality?[100] I think Rabbi Yose avoids that charge, which could be made against God, by taking the root of the verb "pray," *pallel,* to mean "judge" (of which there are a number of parallels in scripture).[101] So when a we judge ourselves, we are *deliberating* within our own mind on what we should do.[102]

This inner deliberation is also imagined in a midrash where God deliberates with himself about creating the world.

> Were I to create the world by means of My quality of mercy [*be-middat rahamim*], sinners would abound; and if by means of My quality of justice [*be-middat ha-din*] the world could not endure. So, I shall create it by both My quality of mercy and My quality of judgment. O' might it be that the world will endure![103]

This inner divine dialogue, as it were, deals with God's *relational* capacity as it makes God's subsequent interactions with the human world possible.[104] God can relate Godself to whoever-is-not-God either mercifully or justly. Humans are to be treated mercifully by God not because we deserve it, but when we confess we don't deserve it we thereby plead for God's mercy nonetheless. Humans are to be treated with strict justice by God, which we do deserve, when we are obstinate in our self-satisfaction; that is, when we arrogantly presume to be as autonomous as God, sinfully abusing our capacity for freedom of choice, a capacity we do not give ourselves. It is a capacity not given to us by anyone other than God.

The midrash says that God is already prepared for how he will respond to human action, the action (either good or bad) that will occasion God's appropriate response thereto. Thus in the New Year's Day (Rosh Hashanah) liturgy, the liturgy of the "Day of Judgment" (*yom ha-din*), one of the prayers concludes by beseeching God to "be gracious (*honenu*) and respond to us, even though we have no good deeds." And the prayer begins by our confessing to God that "we have sinned before You."[105] How God responds to the human situation before him, whether justly or mercifully, depends on God's deliberative judgment of the particularities of that situation. One might call this "divine casuistry."[106]

Now we must ask, What distinguishes "deliberation" from "contemplation" or "meditation"? The difference is that one deliberates about what he or she ought to do in a situation where an intelligent practical decision is called for, and the choice made because of this deliberation is acted on. The whole process of deliberation-decision-choice is the exercise of practical judgment (as we saw earlier). On the other hand, those who say (arguably) that we can contemplate what God is have to admit that such contemplation must be silent.[107] Thus, for Maimonides (the most prominent Jewish proponent of this view), contemplation of God can only be silent because God did not communicate even with Moses (the most direct recipient of revelation) in words.[108] The appropriate response to silent revelation can only be silent contemplation. Contemplation is wordless since our words come from our worldly experience. That is why we can only speak of what God *does* in relation to us but not of what God *is* by Godself. That is what differentiates contemplation (*higgayon* in biblical Hebrew) from intentional thought (*mahshavah*). Contemplation is an inner-mental activity unconnected to action. One mediates silently.[109]

The great eleventh-century French exegete Rashi discusses the question of God's inner dialogue with Godself. It comes in his comment on the scriptural verse "When Moses came to the Tent [of Meeting or *Ohel Mo'ed*], the cloudy pillar would come down, standing at the opening of the Tent; and He spoke with Moses" (Exodus 33:9). Rashi quotes another scriptural verse (also about Moses's contact with God at the *Ohel Mo'ed*), "He [Moses] heard the voice speaking to him" (Numbers 7:89), arguing that God is not talking directly to Moses because "to Him" refers to God speaking with Godself (*beino le-vein atsmo*). An ordinary human (*hedyot*), even Moses, only overhears the inner divine dialogue. In fact, in his comment on Numbers 7:89, Rashi explains that when Moses came to the *Ohel Mo`ed* to speak to God, the transitive verb "speak" (*medabber*) could be read as an intransitive verb: *mitdabber*, namely, "speaking-by-Godself-to-Godself."

Picking up on Rashi's point (no doubt influenced by the Talmud text about God's prayer), the sixteenth-century Italian exegete Obadiah Sforno calls this God's "self-knowledge" (*be-haskilo et atsmo*).[110] Even though Sforno deals with the effects of God's thinking along Neoplatonic lines of one thinking cause having multiple ontological effects, he still does not seem to look upon God's thinking as the kind of intelligent deliberation and free choice involved in practical reasoning.

Now Sforno does not deal with the metaphysical question of what God is thinking about, only that God thinks apart from or prior to God's speaking to humans about matters pertaining to their interrelationship. Perhaps his avoidance of the question of the content of God's thought, which the rabbis did speculate on, is due to the tendency of medieval exegetes to sidestep the philosophical challenge, coming from Muslim critics of biblical-rabbinic theology, who charged that this kind of speculation is too anthropomorphic. As such, it can be easily dismissed by philosophers as being mythological or poetic rather than philosophically insightful.[111] In this critique, the philosophical critics of biblical-rabbinic Judaism employed Aristotelian and Neoplationic philosophy, by whose standards the *Quran*-based theology seems to be more rational than is biblically based theology.[112] Also, in Sforno's intellectual milieu too, any metaphysical speculation had to be done along the lines of Aristotelian and Neoplatonic metaphysics. So when a theological statement did not lend itself to being reworked philosophically, its metaphysical implications had to be explained away.

In fact, this imaginative speculation seems to have embarrassed the tenth-century Egyptian-Babylonian theologian Saadiah Gaon, who was the first major theologian in the rabbinic tradition to deal with the philosophical challenge posed by the Islamic theologians. Replying to the query of an anti-rabbinic Jewish critic of rabbinic anthropomorphism, Saadiah says that this is "hyperbole and allegory" designed to imagine God teaching Israel how to pray by becoming the teacher of prayer itself by divine example to be imitated.[113] And explicitly quoting the rabbinic text about God's praying to Godself, the eleventh-century Babylonian theologian Hai Gaon says that the statement about God's self-prayer was made at the time Moses was being taught by God how to invoke God by calling on God's qualities of mercy and forgiveness.[114] (We shall return to the question of the practical implications of this statement about God's praying shortly.)

DIVINE PATHOS

Abraham Joshua Heschel brilliantly speculated on what it is *in* God's intelligent inwardness, God's wisdom, that enables God to freely relate Godself
to created humankind generally and to the people Israel specifically. He very
much deepens the imaginative insight of Rabbi Yose we have been examining here. This comes out in his theory of divine "pathos." By this bold
term, Heschel means that there is an aspect of God's inner life whereby God
chooses not only to affect the world but also to be affected by the world.[115] As
he memorably put it,

> Pathos was understood not as unreasoned emotion, but as an act formed with
> intention . . . the result of decision and determination. . . . The divine reaction
> to human conduct does not operate automatically. Man's deeds do not neces-
> sitate but only occasion divine pathos. Man is not the immediate but merely the
> incidental cause of pathos in God. . . . The divine pathos is not an absolute force
> which exists regardless of man. . . . [It is] an attitude called forth by man's con-
> duct; a response, not a cause. Man is in a sense an agent, not only the recipient.
> It is within his power to evoke either the pathos of love or the pathos of anger.[116]

In the earliest version of the work just quoted above, Heschel speaks of God's
capacity for relating to humans as the a priori source (*Beziehungsursprung*)
of humans being able to relate to God.[117] In fact, he goes so far as to say that
"pathos is man's place (*Ort*) in God."[118] In between the publication of the
German version and the publication of the English version of *The Prophets*,
Heschel wrote, "The Bible is not man's theology but God's anthropology,
dealing with man and what He asks of him rather than with the nature
of God."[119]

Of course, many find the notion that God is affected by his creatures to
be presumptuous in holding that there is passivity in God.[120] Doesn't this
very much compromise God's self-sufficiency, God's transcendence of any
dependency or contingency? Doesn't this make God less than absolute?
However, there is an essential difference between divine affectivity and that
of creatures, even human creatures who are made in God's image. The difference is that we humans are affective necessarily, that is, by our very nature.
We cannot choose whether or not to to be affected by others, we can only
choose how to react or not react to those others we have been affected by.
That choice is rational when it is the result of deliberation rather than being
an undeliberated reaction. Conversely, God's transcendence is God's absolute
freedom to choose to either be affected by his creatures, or to remain in his
total self-sufficiency altogether. The way God makes that fundamental choice
is unknowable by us. We humans can only speculate as to how God willed

primordially to be related to creatures at all and then how God chooses to relate Godself to us in particular transactions. However, humans who think they can opt out of their affectivity, that is, opt out of their necessary inter-personal relationships (with both fellow humans and with God) are, in fact, imitating the god of Aristotle and not the Lord God of Israel.[121]

Even God's quality of mercy (*middat rahamim*) is properly understood when it is taken to be not only effective but also affective for only the God who is affected by his creatures could effectively respond to them in a way that they feel God is not only acting *for* them but just as much staying *with* them, having been affected *by* them. "When he calls to me, I will answer him; I am with him in affliction [*ve-tsarah*], I will save him for he acknowl-edges My name" (Psalms 91:15).[122] Loving acts (*gemilut hasadim*) are only effective when those being affected by them feel that their affection is due to the affection of the one responding to them by being with them so lov-ingly.[123] Without this affective reciprocity, this emotional give-and-take, love becomes quite impersonal.[124]

This acceptance of divine affectivity helps us to better understand the prob-lematic attribution of anger to God by scripture, which the rabbis deepened by their theological speculation rather than allegorizing it away. Now unlike mercy/love which we regard as admirable in humans, we usually consider anger as a trait to be avoided or overcome.[125] Yet when we view God's anger as being "righteous indignation," which God deliberates on before enacting it, we can understand that just as love needs both action and its accompany-ing feeling in order to truly effect its objects, so does justice need both action and its accompanying feeling to truly effect its objects. In the face of great injustice, we need to sense that the judge is concerned with the plight of the victims, suffering with them, and is deeply disturbed by their plight. As such, the judge should become angry or incensed on their behalf. The victims espe-cially need to sense that God will "avenge the blood of His servants that has been shed" (Psalms 79:10). Indeed, the perpetrators of the injustice need to be frightened by God's anger even though they are those, as T. S. Eliot put it, "who fear the injustice of men less than the justice of God."[126] In such cases, anything less than concerned anger would strongly imply God's indifference.

The opposite of indifference, though, is not blind reaction but rather delib-erately chosen feeling that motivates action. As Heschel declared, "The proph-ets never thought that God's anger is something that cannot be accounted for, unpredictable, irrational. It is never a spontaneous outburst. . . . The anger of God is not a blind, explosive force, operating without reference to the behavior of man, but rather voluntary and purposeful, motivated by concern for right and wrong."[127]

Furthermore, even the perpetrators of injustice are not totally forsaken by God. They can return to God, which is *teshuvah*. That is, they can always repent. "For I do not desire the death of the sinners, says the Lord God, but that they return [*ve-hashivu*] and live" (Ezekiel 18:32). As the rabbis taught, even though sinners may not evade just punishment from a human court by confessing their sin and voicing their contrition, yet if they do that by beseeching God to let their death be atonement for all their sins, they will thereby enjoy God's everlasting favor in the world-yet-to-come (*olam ha-ba*).[128] Ultimately, God's mercy trumps God's anger. Finally, God's mercy "will obliterate death forever" (Isaiah 25:8).[129]

This now leads us to look at the practical ramifications of the text in the Babylonian Talmud about God's prayer for the active human response to God's pathos, epitomized by the biblical prophets, is to sympathize with God's pathos.[130] Since the heart is considered the seat of all feeling, and since prayer is "the heart's service to God" (*avodah she-ba-lev*), prayer is the most intimate way humans can sympathize with God.[131] Note the following:

> Rabbi Ishmael ben Elisha [the High Priest] said that once I entered [the Holy-of-Holies on the Day of Atonement] to offer incense. There I saw God, who said to me, Ishmael my son, bless Me. I said to Him, May it be will that Your mercy subdue your anger, and that Your mercy will surge so that You will judge their [Israel] case above and beyond the strict letter of the law [*lifnim mi-shurat ha-din*].[132]

Now in dealing with both parts of the text, being embarrassed by its anthropomorphism, Saadiah Gaon (followed by many subsequent rationalists) saw the second statement (just quoted above) about human prayer to God as primary and the first statement about God's prayer to Godself as secondary. He says that "in many places in Scripture, the Maker [*ha-po'el*] is compared to what is made [*la-pa'ul*]." In Saadiah's view, the rabbis speaking in this Talmud text are doing what scripture does when speaking about God.[133]

However (and I think this is consistent with Heschel's theory), it is more accurate to call this text an expression of "theomorphism" rather than calling it "anthropomorphism."[134] In other words, isn't it theologically more profound to speculate that humans are to imitate God's inner prayer rather than imagining God as exemplifying how humans are to pray to him? For what assurance do humans have that God cares about our prayerful requests unless we speculate (by inferring from God's interactions with us that have been revealed to us) that God is prepared beforehand to respond to our requests made thereafter? That is because our concerns are already God's concerns, and aspects of God's inner life are employed in God's deliberations as to how to relate to his humans creatures when we call upon him. Human creatures are to imitate the divine Creator. God is more than an exemplar. Thus when God says to Rabbi Ishmael, "Bless Me," God is asking Rabbi Ishmael to pray to God as God prays to Godself.

Finally, there are implications of this *imitatio Dei* not only for the divine-human relationship but just as much for interhuman relationships. Thus the scriptural statement of God being "merciful and gracious" [*rahum ve-hanun*] (Exodus 34:6) has two distinct (though interconnected) functions for the rabbis. In terms of the divine-human relationship, Hai Gaon (quoted earlier) sees the rabbinic statement of God's prayer to Godself as warranted by God's revealing his mercy and grace to Israel in scripture. This mercy and grace can be invoked especially when the forgiveness of sin is called for. And in terms of interhuman relationships, the second-century sage Abba Saul comments on the verse "This is my God and I shall glorify Him [*v'anvehu*]" (Exodus 15:2) by taking the word *v'anvehu* to mean "I and He" (*ani ve-hu*). He then concludes that one is to "be like Him [God]" (*hevei domeh lo*). Just as God is gracious and merciful, so you [humans] are to be gracious and merciful."[135] To whom? To each other!

To understand this bold midrash, we should remember that scripture does not say here that God "acts mercifully and graciously" (*rahem ve-honen*) but that God has the capacity for mercy and grace even before God actually acts mercifully and graciously. Thus humans, created in the image and likeness (*demut*) of God, are capable of acting mercifully and graciously with one another because we have been given this analogous capacity. Unlike God, though, we humans do not know we have this capacity until after we have exercised it and have been informed by God's revelation that it is not originally ours. It is originally God's alone. We can only speculate that God knows it before actually exercising it.

Imitation of God's grace and God's mercy is learned from what we heard in the Talmud text we have been long examining, especially God's direction to Godself, which is then to be claimed of God by his people Israel. Israel's claim upon God is for God to deal with us "above and beyond the strict letter of the law" (*lifnim mi-shurat ha-din*). In Jewish law, this refers to a judge who forgives or foregoes the full claim of one party against another party in a civil suit.[136] In fact, even before the case is adjudicated, the judge should encourage the parties to compromise (*pesharah*) so that each party agrees not to fully claim what he or she believes is their right.[137] God is to be imitated in this virtuous human interaction for the sake of the covenantal relationship by our not exacting strict justice from each other. Thus we human parties to the covenant should not fully claim from one another what we believe we justly deserve. This is for the sake of the common good (*bonum commune*), which in biblical parlance is God's "covenant of peace" (*briti shalom*—Numbers

25:12). Acting for the sake of the common good is supposed to overcome acting for one's private interests when these interests conflict with that good.[138]

The idea of compromise as *imitatio Dei* comes out in the liturgy of Yom Kippur, the Day of Atonement, when the Jewish people seek reconciliation with God. In one medieval Yom Kippur hymn, there is the refrain "Look to the covenant [*la-brit habet*] and not to our [bad] inclinations."[139] In other words, "God, forgive our human transgressions for the sake of our unbroken relationship with you!" So too are we to look to our lesser interpersonal relationships to reflect God's greater relationship with us.

From these interpretations of God's mercy and of God's justice, the connection of the inner aspect and the outer aspect of the life of God, we human creatures who are the recipients of revelation can imitate the connection of the inner aspects and the outer aspects of the God's life. That is why theologians are justified in speculating what this connection is and what it means for human action in this world. Such speculation is to be encouraged when it enables us to deepen our relationship with God and with our fellow humans before God in the world. Such speculation is only to be discouraged when it takes one out of the world where we interact with God along with our fellow humans, fueling our desire to love and be loved by God exclusively. As the English poet W. H. Auden put it so profoundly, "for the error bred in the bone of each woman and each man craves what it cannot have, not universal love, but to be loved alone."[140]

NOTES

1. See Kant, *Critique of Pure Reason*, B737–43.

2. Re God, see e.g., Ps. 40:6. Re humans, see e.g., Prov. 16:3. Cf. MT: Teshuvah, 5.5 re Isa. 55:8.

3. The rabbis called deliberate action "thoughtful work" (*mele'khet mahshevet*), see B. Betsah 13b; Hagigah 10b. Intention is called "direction" (*kavvanah*) as in M. Berakhot 2.1; M. Rosh Hashanah 3.7; B. Kidushin 40a re Isa. 3:10. See, also, G. E. M. Anscombe, *Intention*, 2nd ed. (Ithaca, NY: Cornell University Press, 1963), esp. sec. 16. For *kavvanah* in rabbinic terminology as the equivalent of *mahshavah* in biblical terminology, see Alexander Kohut, *Arukh ha-Shalem* (Tel Aviv: Shilo, 1970), 4:206b–7a; MT: Shabbat, 1.9.

4. Plato, *Apology*, 29A.

5. For the insistence that speculation as to what God is thinking, seeming to be wild imagination, still having to be able to be connected somehow to a scriptural text stating what God has said or done, see B. Avodah Zarah 54b and Rashi, s.v. "ela," referring to *Tanhuma*: Naso, sec. 6 re Deut. 32:18, ed. Buber, 29.

6. For a brilliant discussion of all this, see David Weiss Halivni, *Revelation Restored* (New York: Routledge, 2018).

7. MT: Yesodei ha-Torah, 4.12 re B. Sukkah 28a.

8. Taken by itself, "I am what I am" is a tautology. Translating it as "I am who I am" is no better. Thus Hermann Cohen writes that the translation *Ich bin wer ich bin* is "scarcely intelligible, if not meaningless," explicitly referring to Emil Kautzsch's *Die Heilige Schrift des Alten Testaments* (Freiburg: J. C. B. Mohr Siebeck, 1896) in *Religion of Reason Out of the Sources of Judaism*, trans. S. Kaplan (New York: Frederick Ungar, 1972), 42.

9. *Proslogion*, chap. 3, in *St. Anselm: Basic Writings*, trans. S. N. Deane (La Salle, IL: Open Court, 1962), 54–55: "It is possible to conceive of a being which cannot be conceived not to exist. . . . To thee alone, therefore, it belongs to exist more truly, and hence to a higher degree than all others." Citing Anselm is pertinent to Jewish theology because Anselm's treatise is a response to "the fool (*naval)* who says in his heart, there is no God (*ein elohim*; Ps. 53:2)." Following the Vulgate, Anselm designates *naval* as *insipiens*, one who denies God theoretically. But in rabbinic tradition, *naval* is one who denies God's concern for his or her practice by presuming God doesn't care for what this person does, as indicated in v. 3. See *Midrash Tehillim*, 53.1, ed. Buber, 287–88. Nevertheless, both theoretical and practical denial deny God as the Absolute (see for example Isa. 43:10, 44:6).

10. The Vulgate translates *ehyeh asher ehyeh* as *Ego sum qui sum . . . Qui est.* Thomas Aquinas, *Summa Theologiae* I, q. 13, a. 11, quotes the eighth-century church father John of Damascus (*de Fide Orthodoxa*, 1.9) in a Latin translation that employs the Vulgate's rendition of Exod. 3:14 (*quae de Deo dicuntur nomibus, est qui est*). This is elaborated by modern Thomists such as Étienne Gilson, *The Spirit of Mediaeval Philosophy*, trans. A. H. C. Downes (London: Sheed and Ward, 1936), 51–54; *God and Philosophy*, 2nd ed. (New Haven, CT: Yale University Press, 2002), 62–63; also Thomas Weinandy, *Does God Suffer?* (Notre Dame, IN: University of Notre Dame Press, 2004), 77; and Matthew Levering, *Scripture and Metaphysics* (Oxford: Blackwell, 2004), 61.

11. *Wisdom of Solomon* 13:1.

12. *Quod Deterius*, 44.160. See how LXX to Gen. 1:26 renders the Hebrew *be-tsalmenu* as *kat' eikona hēmeteran* in Greek. Also, the *Quran* (28:31) emphasizes God's telling Moses of his self-sufficiency.

13. See Thomas Aquinas, *Commentary on the Sentences of Peter Lombard*, Prologue, q. 1, a. 2 ad 2.

14. Maimonides, *Guide of the Perplexed*, 1.63, trans. S. Pines (Chicago: University of Chicago Press, 1963), 155. For the heavy influence of the Muslim philosopher Ibn Sina (Avicenna) on Maimonides's notions of essence and existence, see L. E. Goodman, *Avicenna* (London and New York: Routledge, 1992), 58–79.

15. Maimonides, *Guide of the Perplexed*, 1.64, 156. For Judah Halevi, the Tetragrammaton is God's only proper name. See *Kuzari*, 4.1–3. This point has been recently developed by Protestant theologian R. Kendall Soulen, *Irrevocable* (Minneapolis, MN: Fortress Press, 2022), esp., 23–27.

16. Some have held that Maimonides considered *ehyeh asher ehyeh* to be one of the proper names of God (MT: Yesodei ha-Torah, 6.2 re B. Shevuot 35a, and Karo, *Kesef Mishneh* thereon).

17. *Posterior Analytics*, 2.1/89b23–34.

18. See T. F. Torrance, *Divine and Contingent Order* (Oxford: Oxford University Press, 1981).

19. For Plato there is a category called "godliness" or "divinity" (*to theion*) through which the individual gods (*theoi*) have their divine identity (*Phaedrus*, 246E–248A). For Aristotle, "the God" (*ho theos*) is the chief member of the class "divinity" (*Metaphysics*, 12.7/1072b25–35; *Nicomachean Ethics*, 10.7/1177a15–20). Nevertheless, the difference between "God" and "gods" is one of degree rather than one of kind.

20. See M. Berakhot 5.3; B. Berakhot 33b.

21. *Metaphysics*, 12.9/1074b20–35.

22. T. S. Eliot, *Murder in the Cathedral*, in *The Complete Poems and Plays: 1909–1950* (New York: Harcourt, Brace & World, 1971), 220.

23. See E. Jacobson, "The Future of Kabbalah," in *Kabbalah and Modernity*, ed. B. Huss, M. Pasi, and K. von Stuckand (Leiden: Brill, 2010), 58–62.

24. See Gershom Scholem, *Major Trends in Jewish Mysticism*, 3rd rev. ed. (New York: Schocken Books, 1961), 205–43; Gershom Scholem, *On the Kabbalah and Its Symbolism*, trans. R. Manheim (New York: Schocken Books, 1969), 94–109.

25. *Zohar*: Va-yetsei, 1:156a and Korah, 3:178b re Deut. 4:35.

26. See Charles Hartshorne and W. L. Reese, *Philosophers Speak of God* (Chicago: University of Chicago Press, 1987), 499–514.

27. See Gershom Scholem, *Origins of the Kabbalah*, trans. A. Arkush (Princeton, NJ: Princeton University Press, 1987), 423–26.

28. Like Kabbalah, the Septuagint was seen to be divine revelation by Greek-speaking or Hellenistic Jews, in whose synagogues the Septuagint was read and interpreted as Torah. See Philo, *De Vita Mosis*, 7.37–40.

29. See Aristotle, *Metaphysics*, 3.3/99b20; 4.1/1003b24; 7.1/1028b5; 12.10/1075b34.

30. *Zohar*: Aharei-mot, 3:65b, trans. Daniel Matt (Stanford, CA: Stanford University Press, 2018), 7:429.

31. In his superb translation (7:429, n. 222), Matt speaks of this "channeling" (*l'amshakha*) as "emanating." Indeed for the kabbalists, *yesh m'ayin* ("something from nothing," like *ex nihilo*) means that finite entities (*yesh*) emanate from the Infinite (*ein sof*, literally "without end"). The relative negation *ayin* (like *mē* in Greek) instead of the more absolute *lo* (like *ou* or *ouk* in Greek) now negates finitude rather than negating being. So as a double negative it denotes the very opposite of Nothingness even though the transcendent reality to which it alludes cannot be named even by the Tetragrammaton. Unlike Philo et al., this emantion is *ad intra*, that is, taking place within the Godself. It is not *ad extra*, that is, it doesn't move from God into what is not-God. See *Zohar*: Haazinu, 3:288b; Bo, 2:42b re Isa. 40:18; Joseph Gikatila, *Shaarei Orah*, chap. 5, ed. Ben-Shlomo (Jerusalem: Mosad Bialik, 1981), 189–90.

32. Sometimes the rabbis speak of God keeping commandments (Y. Rosh Hashanah 1.3/57a–b re Lev. 18:30 and 19:32). But that is God's choice to become exemplary in God's covenantal relationship with Israel. It is not Israel's participation in God's life.

33. B. Baba Metsia 59b re Deut. 30:12.

34. See Scholem, *On the Kabbalah*, 122–35.

35. Nevertheless, there have been considerable conflicts between kabbalistic interpreters of Halakhah and non-kabbalistic and even anti-kabbalistic interpreters. There has been the persistent suspicion that the kabbalists are crypto-antinomians. See Jacob Katz, *Halakhah ve-Kabbalah* (Jerusalem: Magnes Press, 1986), 9–101.

36. Maimonides, *Guide of the Perplexed*, 1.71 attributes Christian trintarianism (along with some Muslim and even some Jewish theological errors) to the influence of ancient Greek anti-philosophical traditions. For extensive discussion of Jewish anti-trinitarianism, see Samuel Krauss, "Trinity" in *Jewish Encyclopedia* (1905) 12:260–61.

37. MT: Yesodei ha-Torah, 1.7.

38. *Teshuvot ha-Rivash* (Lemberg, 1805), no. 157.

39. Saadiah, *Book of Beliefs and Opinions*, 1.3; Maimonides, *Guide of the Perplexed*, 1.52.

40. Along these lines, Kant (*Critique of Pure Reason*, B370–71) criticized Plato for turning functional concepts into ideas, which are supersensible entities (*eidoi*). In the same way, Hermann Cohen criticized both Philo and Christianity for their respective hypostatizing of logos, turning God's speech (*dibbur*) into a divine entity. See Cohen, *Religion of Reason*, 238–39.

41. The locus classicus is found in Plotinus, *Enneads*, 5.2, where emanation is termed "overflow" (*hypererryē*), which became *al-fits* in Arabic and *hashpa'ah* in Hebrew (see Maimonides, *Guide of the Perplexed*, 1.46, 2.37). "Emanation" comes from the Latin *emanoare* ("to flow").

42. The best explication of all this is found in I. Tishby, *Mishnat ha-Zohar*, 2nd ed. (Jerusalem: Mosad Bialik, 1957), 1:95–117. See also Meir ibn Gabbai, *Avodat ha-Qodesh*, 1.2 and 1.12.

43. *Teshuvot ha-Rivash*, no. 157.

44. In rabbinic teaching, God can and does contract his Indwelling Presence (*metsamtsem shekhinato*) into the Ark of the Covenant in the Temple but without sacrificing his capacity to transcend any definite place in the world (*Tanhuma*: Vayaqhel, no. 7 re Exod. 37:1, Jer. 23:24, Josh. 3:11). Unlike the kabbalistic idea of *tsimtsum* as an internal divine process, the use by the rabbis of the verb *tsamstem* denotes God's mode of externally relating infinite Godself to finite creatures in their places in this world.

45. See Gershom Scholem's classic essay "Schöpfung aus Nichts und Selbstverschränkung Gottes," *Eranos Jahrbuch* (1956), 25:87–119. Cf. D. Novak, "Self-Contraction of the Godhead in Kabbalistic Theology" in *Neoplatonism and Judaism*, ed. L. E. Goodman (Albany: SUNY Press, 1992), 299–318.

46. The Hebrew verb *bar'o* ("create") in scripture is primarily predicated of God alone since primordial creation is a unique divine property (see for example Isa. 42:5). Since at least the second century BCE, though, *borē* has denoted God as *Creator ex nihilo*. See II Macc. 7:28; also D. Novak, *Athens and Jerusalem* (Toronto: University of Toronto Press, 2019), 118–23 and 339, nn. 43–44). But the verb *bar'o* has a more mundane meaning, viz., "clear out" as in Josh. 17:15, "Go up to the forest and there you shall make a clearing for yourself (*u-bere'ta lekha*). . . . Because the mountain of Ephraim is too cramped (*ats lekha*) for you." Martin Buber (with Franz Rosenzweig)

in *Das Buch Jehoschua* (Berlin: Verlag Lambert Schneider, n.d.), 69, translates this phrase *hau es dir heraus* ("hew it out for yourself"). Thus by creating an outside, one demarcates one's inside (see for example B. Zevahim 15b). This type of mundane creation, which we humans can experience in the world, is the closest we can come to understanding by analogy God's primordial creation. We can speculate that by making a world outside Godself God has thereby demarcated his inside by differentiation. In fact, the Aramaic *br'ai* ("outside") is a cognate of the Hebrew *bar'o* (see for example B. Temurah 11a).

47. See *Mishnat ha-Zohar*, 1:381–90.

48. See *Ethics* I, Appendix; H. A. Wolfson, *Spinoza* (Cambridge, MA: Harvard University Press, 1934), 1:96–111.

49. Cohen, *Religion of Reason*, 39–40. And whereas the identification of God-as-Being *and* the cosmos, for Cohen, led to pantheism (which is incompatible with the Hebraic notion of creation), he nevertheless sides with Parmenides who "combatted the error" that Cohen sees as stemming from Xenophon onward (ibid., 3.12, 66–67).

50. Hermann Cohen, *Der Begriff der Religion im System der Philosophie* (Giessen: A. Töpelmann, 1915), 47. This book was the last book Cohen himself published before his death in 1918. *Religion of Reason* was published posthumously by his widow in 1919.

51. Cohen, *Religion of Reason,* 42–48. For the relation of *Sein* and *Werden*, before its theological application in *Religion of Reason* (1919), see his 1902 *Logik der reinen Erkenntnis*, 2.3, 12, *Werke*, ed. H. Holzhey (Hildesheim: Georg Olms Verlag, 1977), 6:122, 134.

52. Cohen, *Religion of Reason*, 35. Thus Becoming can never merge with Being, not even aspiring to be absorbed into Being, because that would realize (*verwirklichen*) what can only be ideal, that is, unrealizable. As such, the dialectical tension between Being and Becoming can never and ought never actually be united. This is very different from Aristotle (*Nicomachean Ethics*, 10.7/1177b26–1178a4), who holds (and all who have followed him) that humans can strive to be-come like God (in a kind of *unio mystica*). Although this union is quite rare, it is an attainable goal (*telos*) for true philosophers nonetheless. That is because God is the most real (*ens realissimum*), the most perfect Being, who is to be found at the apex and acting as the supremely attractive *telos* of a finite cosmos. That cosmic finitude makes the gulf between God and not-God bridgeable, even if only for very few humans. But, for Cohen, Being and Becoming interact dialectically in an infinite universe where, like parallel lines in Euclidean geometry, they can never meet.

53. Cohen, *Religion of Reason*, 59–70.

54. Translated according to Abraham Ibn Ezra: *kemo atsmekha*, as in v. 22.

55. Maimonides, *Guide of the Perplexed*, 1.38. Nevertheless, it would seem that for Maimonides, God's imitable goodness is generally learned from God's beneficent providence in nature, rather than from God's specific revelation in history (3.54 re Jer. 9:23).

56. B. Sotah 14a re Deut. 4:24.

57. B. Shabbat 133b re Exod. 15:2.

58. Cohen, *Religion of Reason,* 307–8. As such, humans can only approximate the ideal, that is, progress toward it yet never achieve it. That assumes, though, that history has an upward trajectory. Surely the aftermath of World War II, near the end of which Cohen died, convinced many who had been idealists before the war that there was no such upward historical trajectory at all. If anything, history had gone downward or nowhere.

59. Y. Yevamot 15.2/14d re Ps. 140:8; note of Abraham ben David of Posquières (Ravad) to MT: Teshuvah, 8.8.

60. The translation here follows the invocation of this verse on B. Berakhot 34b.

61. For the condemnation of those who believe they can calculate the end-time, much less actually bring it about by their own efforts, see B. Sanhedrin 97b re Isa. 30:18.

62. See B. Sanhedrin 97b re Isa. 30:18; also D. Novak, *Zionism and Judaism* (Cambridge: Cambridge University Press, 2015), 228–40.

63. B. Berakhot 4a re Ps. 27:13–14.

64. Martin Buber with Franz Rosenzweig, *Die Fünf Bücher der Weisung* (Cologne: Jakob Hegner, 1954), 158. Re *dasein,* note Buber's translation of Isa. 43:10 as *nicht wird, nach mir es dasein, doch ich, doch ICH BIN DA,* in *Das Buch Yeschayahu* (Berlin: Schocken Verlag, n.d.), 175. Also note his translation of Ezek. 35:10 as *und Er war doch dort da* in *Das Buch Yecheskel* (Berlin: Schocken Verlag, n.d.), 164.

65. Of course many students of twentieth-century philosophy will assume that Martin Heidegger introduced this new usage of *dasein* in his 1927 work *Sein und Zeit,* and that Heidegger's usage influenced Buber's and Rosenzweig's translation of Exod. 3:14. However, already in 1925 Buber and Rosenzweig were writing their Bible translation in which they used *dasein* in this novel way. See Martin, Buber, *Zu einer neuen Verdeutschung der Schrift* (Olten: Jakob Hegner Verlag, 1954), 37. Furthermore, in his 1938 inaugural lecture at the Hebrew University in Jerusalem ("Was ist der Mensch?"), Martin Buber (newly arrived there as a refugee from Germany, where Heidegger was the most prominent philosopher) very much emphasized his differences with Heidegger regarding *dasein.* See Martin Buber, "What is Man?" in *Between Man and Man,* trans. R. G. Smith (Boston: Beacon Press, 1955), 163–81. Also see D. Novak, "Buber's Critique of Heidegger," *Modern Judaism* (1985) 5:125–40.

66. Kant, *Critique of Pure Reason,* B626.

67. Kant, *Critique of Pure Reason,* B276. This is what Kant called a "synthetic proposition," where the object cannot be deduced from the subject as can be done in an "analytic proposition" (ibid., B11–14). Hence their relation is external to each of them rather than being internal to one of the two parties or being interned within a third party. The object is more than a definition of the subject so one cannot go through the subject to reach what is subsumed within it. And both the subject and the object are not defined as components of a system. Any such system would mediate between two of its particula. In other words, one cannot know anything about what a point on a grid does unless one locates that point's position on the grid first. The subject and the object, though, are directly (*unmittelbar*) related to each other.

68. When God is actually present to fulfill his promise to be present with his people, God says *hinneni*. See Isa. 52:6 and 58:9, and David Kimhi's (Radak) comments on both these verses.

69. In the two places in the Talmud (B. Shabbat 10a re Exod. 18:13 and Gen. 1:5; B. Shabbat 119b re Gen. 1:31) where partnership with God is asserted, the text says that humans who cooperate with God in the ongoing task of creation are "as if (*k'ilu*) they had been made a partner (*shuttaf*) of God." Ordinarily "partnership" (*shuttfut*) is a relationship between equals (MT: Shluhin ve-Shuttfut, 6.1–2). See D. Novak, *Jewish Social Ethics* (New York: Oxford University Press, 1992), 223–24.

70. B. Kiddushin 42b and B. Baba Kama 56a.

71. See for example Umberto Cassuto, *A Commentary on the Book of Exodus*, trans. I. Abrahams (Jerusalem: Magnes Press, 1967), 36–37; Nahum M. Sarna, *The JPS Torah Commentary: Exodus* (Philadelphia: Jewish Publication Society, 1991), 18; Carol Meyers, *Exodus* (Cambridge: Cambridge University Press, 2005), 57.

72. It is reported (Y. Yoma 3.7/40d) that by the first century CE, when the high priest blessed the people in the Jerusalem Temple on Yom Kippur, his pronunciation of God's name would be so garbled that it couldn't be repeated. The reason given for this unusual practice (cf. M. Sotah 7.6) is that there was great concern that an increasing number of disreputable persons would misuse the name (B. Kiddushin 71a and Rashi, s.v. "mi-she-rabbu;" also see M. Sanhedrin 10.1; *Shemot Rabbah* 3.7). So it seems there were Jews then who still held the ancient pagan belief that knowing a god's name would give them magical powers.

73. For the close connection of these two words having the same two identical consonants, note the play on words in Ezek. 48:35: "And the named (*ve-shem*) of the city from that day on shall be 'The Lord is there'(*shammah*)." See Ezek. 35:10; Zech. 14:9. For *shem* as one's address, see Ps. 49:12 and Rashi thereon re Gen. 4:17; see also Abraham Ibn Ezra's comment on Ps. 49:12.

74. Thus before speaking to others, one first locates them by calling their name or address to indicate that this is the person one is addressing oneself to. See *Sifra*, ed. Weiss, 3c; B. Yoma 4b; *Shemot Rabbah* 19.3 re Lev. 1:1.

75. *Beresheet Rabbah* 53.14 (and n. 8, ed. Theodor-Albeck, 572–73); Y. Rosh Hashanah 1.3/57a; B. Rosh Hashanah 15b re Gen. 21:17.

76. *Beresheet Rabbah* 68.9 re Gen. 28:11 (and n. 1, ed. Theodor-Albeck, 777–78). Note how God says (Hosea 5:15), "I shall go to My place (*el meqomi*)," which Rashi paraphrases "I shall depart from them and return to heaven," that is, go back to another world altogether. Following Rashi, David Kimhi (Radak) thereon calls heaven "the place of Myself (*meqom kevodi*)."

77. Cohen, *Religion of Reason*, 71.

78. B. Yevamot 49b and Rashi, s.v. "be-himats'o."

79. All of this is counter to the Jewish rationalist tradition enunciated by Saadiah Gaon, Ibn Ezra, and Maimonides. See Saadiah Gaon, *Commentary on the Torah*: Exod. 3:14, ed. and trans. Y. Kafih (Jerusalem: Mosad ha-Rav Kook, 1963), 50; Abraham Ibn Ezra, *Commentary on the Torah*: Exod. 3:14, ed. A. Weiser (Jerusalem: Mosad ha-Rav Kook, 1977), 31–32; Maimonides, *Guide of the Perplexed*, 1.61. For a similar countering of the Catholic rationalist tradition, specifically re

Exod. 3:14, by a contemporary Catholic philosopher, see Jean-Luc Marion, *God Without Being*, trans. T. A. Carlson (Chicago: University of Chicago Press, 1991), 45, 73.

80. This comes out in the Greek translation of *ehyeh asher ehyeh* by Aquila, a disciple of Rabbi Akivah, in *Origenes Hexaplorum*, ed. F. Field (Oxford: Clarendon Press, 1875), 1:85, viz., *esomai hos esomai* ("I shall be what I shall be"). No doubt Aquila was aware that his translation is contrary to LXX's *eimi ho ōn*.

81. *Kuzari*, 1.25 re Exod. 20:2. This quote is from a translation of the original Judaeo-Arabic of *Kuzari* by Barry Kogan. I thank Alexander Green for obtaining a copy of the typescript of this translation. It is hoped this new English translation will eventually be published. The 1905 English translation by Hartwig Hirschfeld has long been found wanting.

82. See for example Y. Pesahim 10.4/37d re Exod. 13:8.

83. See for example Y. Rosh Hashanah 1.3/57a–b re Lev. 22:9 and *Devarim Rabbah*: Nitsavim, 3rd ed. re Deut. 6:25, ed. Lieberman, 116.

84. M. Berakhot 9.1 and B. Berakhot 54a; M. Kiddushin 1.9 and Y. Kiddushin 1.8/61c re Deut. 11:17–18; T. Berakhot 1.10 re Jer. 23:7–8 and MT: Melakhim, 8.11 re T. Sanhedrin 13.2 and B. Sanhedrin 105a re Ps. 9:18.

85. Much earlier than Rosenzweig, the thirteenth-century halakhist-theologian Nahmanides (Ramban) was also heavily influenced by Halevi as witnessed by his insistence that the twice daily recitation of the *Shema*, viz., "Hear O' Israel, the Lord is our God, the Lord is unique (*eḥad*)" (Deut. 6:4) is only rabbinically mandated whereas the greater scriptural mandate is the prayer *emet ve-yatsiv* that directly follows it because it enunciates the Exodus from Egypt. *Torat Hashem Temimah* in *Kitvei Ramban* 1, ed. C. B. Chavel (Jerusalem: Mosad Harav Kook, 1963), 1:150 re B. Berakhot 21a. See D. Novak, *The Theology of Nahmanides—Systematically Presented* (Atlanta, GA: Scholar's Press, 1992), 33–39.

86. Martin Buber, *Werkausgabe*, ed. C. Wiese (Gütersloh: Gütersloher Verlaghaus, 2019), 13.1:712–16. See also Martin Buber, *Kingship of God*, 3rd rev. ed., trans. R. Scheimann (New York: Harper & Row, 1967), 105–6.

87. Martin Buber, *Werkausgabe*, ed. R. HaCohen (Gütersloh: Gütersloher Verlaghaus, 2012), 14:207–8.

88. *Shemot Rabbah,* 3.5.

89. B. Baba Batra 25a re Neh. 9:6.

90. In some places, *kol* could mean "any." See *Sifra*: Vayiqra 12, ed. Weiss, 11d; B. Menahot 58a re Lev. 2:11; MT: Isurei Mizbeah, 5.1.

91. *Bemidbar Rabbah* 12.4 re Exod. 3:4 (as interpreted by Rabban Gamliel); *Pesiqta de-Rav Kahana*, chap. 1, ed. Mandelbaum, 4. Along these lines, see Y. Berakhot 4.5/8c re Hos. 5:15 and I Kings 9:3.

92. This is more in line with the interpretation of Exod. 40:35 in *Bemidbar Rabbah*, 12.4 by Rabbi Joshua of Sikhnin in the name of Rabbi Levi.

93. *Tanhuma*: Ha'azinu, no. 9 re Isa. 5:6.

94. Franz Rosenzweig, *The Star of Redemption*, trans. B. E. Galli (Madison: University of Wisconsin Press, 2005), 30–48.

95. Buber's and Rosenzweig's contemporary, Christian theologian Karl Barth (d. 1968), interpreted Exod. 3:14 in much the same way as they did. "The translation,

'I am who truly is' [*Ich bin der wahrhaft Seiende*] has been attempted in the light of the LXX [*ego eimi ho ōn*], but it is quite impossible in this context. . . . The I who gives Himself to be known in that he exists as the I of the Lord and therefore acts only as a He and can be called upon only as a Thou in His action, without making Himself known in his I-ness [*Ichheit*]." Karl Barth, *Church Dogmatics*, 2.1.25, trans. G. W. Bromiley (Edinburgh: T. & T. Clark, 2009), 58–59. Barth's notion of God's "I-ness" is a good term for God's inwardness, which is not exhausted by God's exteriority as it is not totally correlated with it. (Let it be remembered that both Karl Barth and Franz Rosenzweig were students of Hermann Cohen, who strived to overcome their teacher's philosophically rigorous God-idea.)

96. See Rosenzweig, *The Star of Redemption*, 69–70.

97. B. Berakhot 7a.

98. This is the case even though some Gentiles pray to the Lord God whether due to Jewish influence or independent of it (B. Menahot 110a re Mal. 1:11).

99. M. Berakhot 9.4.

100. Maimonides, *Guide of the Perplexed*, 3.26 criticizes those who would ascribe to God the irrational characteristics they would normally abhor in a human ruler.

101. See for example Gen. 48:11 and Rashi's comment thereon; B. Yoma 87a re I Sam. 2:25.

102. Even though it is assumed that God is best able to judge unilaterally (see M. Avot. 4.8; also, Y. Sotah 9.10/24a), perhaps to speak of God as an exemplar to human judges, God is imagined to consult with his heavenly court in his practical deliberations concerning what to do to humans whose deeds he is judging (Y. Sanhedrin 1.1/18a re I Kings 22:23).

103. *Beresheet Rabbah* 12.15 re Gen. 2:4, where the two main names for the deity in scripture are employed, viz., YHVH (called *adonai*, i.e., "the Lord"), and *elohim* ("God"). In rabbinic exegesis, the Tetragrammaton usually denotes God's mercy, and *elohim* usually denotes God's justice. See A. Marmorstein, *The Old Rabbinic Doctrine of God* (London: Oxford University Press, 1927),17–53.

104. For rabbinic speculation about options God could have thoughtfully rejected (*alah be-maḥshavah le-fanai*), see B. Menahot 29b; *Beresheet Rabbah* 44.23 re Gen. 15:19; also, B. Eruvin 18a re Gen. 5:2 and *Tos.*, s.v. "bi-shloma"; B. Ketubot 8a and *Tos.*, s.v. "*ḥada be-yetsirah*.

105. Text from *The Koren Mahzor*: Yamim Noraim (Jerusalem: Koren, 2018), 407, 771.

106. B. Rosh Hashanah 16b re Gen. 21:17 and *Beresheet Rabbah* 53.14. For the recommendation of casuistry to human judges, see M. Avot 1.1 and 4.7 and Maimonides's comment thereon; MT: Sanhedrin, 20:7 re Job 29:16.

107. MT: Tefillah, 4.16 re M. Berakhot 5.1; Maimonides, *Guide of the Perplexed*, 1.59 re Ps. 4:5 and 1.59 re Ps. 65:2. For a precedent, see Y. Berakhot 9.1/12d re Ps. 65:2.

108. Maimonides, *Guide of the Perplexed*, 1.65. For a halakhic corollary to this view of wordless revelation, see *Teshuvot ha-Rambam*, ed. Blau, no. 282, 1:331–35 re B. Berakhot 11b.

109. Ps. 19:15.

110. Obadiah Sforno, *Commentary on the Torah*, ed. Z. Gottlieb (Jerusalem: Mosad ha-Rav Kook, 1980), 267.

111. For the denigration of poetry (in which the Bible abounds) when compared to philosophy, see Plato, *Republic*, 599E–601B; also, Maimonides, *Commentary on the Mishnah*: Sanhedrin 10.1, ed. Kafih, 140–41; Maimonides, *Guide of the Perplexed*, 1.59; Maimonides, *Teshuvot ha-Rambam*, ed. Blau, 2:465–66.

112. See Z. Ali Shah, *Anthropomorphic Depictions of God* (London: International Institute of Islamic Thought, 2012).

113. *Otsar ha-Geonim*: B. Berakhot 7a, no. 28, ed. B. M. Lewin, 14–15.

114. *Otsar ha-*Geonim, no. 24 re B. Rosh Hashanah 17b, 12.

115. For the rabbinic view that God is favorably affected by humans intending to please Him, see B. Berakhot 17a; B. Zevahim 46a re Lev. 1:9, 1:17, 2:2; M. Menahot 13.11; B. Menahot 104b re Lev. 2:1 and 110a re Lev. 19:5.

116. Abraham Joshua Heschel, *The Prophets* (Philadelphia: Jewish Publication Society of America, 1962), 224–25. See D. Novak, "Heschel's Phenomenology of Revelation," in *Abraham Joshua Heschel: Philosophy, Theology, and Interreligious Dialogue*, ed. S. Krajewski and A. Lypszyc (Wiesbaden: Harrassowitz Verlag, 2009), 53–76.

117. Abraham Joshua Heschel, *Die Prophetie* (Warsaw: Polish Academy of Sciences, 1936), 180.

118. Heschel, *Die Prophetie*, 182–83. Heschel's use of the term "a priori" follows Kant. It is the capacity in the mind of knowers that enables them to experience the external world intelligently. See *Critique of Pure Reason*, Bx.

119. Abraham Joshua Heschel, *Man Is Not Alone* (New York: Jewish Publication Society of America, 1951), 29; Abraham Joshua Heschel, *God in Search of Man* (New York: Farrar, Straus & Cudahy, 1955), 412–13.

120. The noun *pathos* comes from the Greek verb *pathein* meaning to "be affected" or to "suffer." In German (the language in which Heschel first formulated his theory of divine pathos) *pathos* is internal reflexive experience called *Erlebnis*, which is distinct from the reflective experience of the external world called *Erfahrung*.

121. Cf. Plato, *Nicomachean Ethics*, 10.7–8/1177b25-1178a25; also Maimonides, *Guide of the Perplexed*, 3.51.

122. *Mekhilta*: Bo re Isa. 63:9, ed. Horovitz-Rabin, 51. See also Y. Rosh Hashanah 1.3/57a re Ps. 103:10, Prov. 30:31; and Fraenkel, *Qorban ha`Edah*, s.v. "zarzir;" *Beresheet Rabbah* 49.7 re Gen. 18:22, ed. Theodor-Albeck, 505 and n. 4 thereon.

123. See MT: Evel, 14.1 re Lev. 19:18.

124. This mutual erotic affection or affecting is dealt with extensively by the kabbalists in their differentiation and relation of the God-human relationship involving both *it`aruta de-l`ela* ("awakening from above"), viz., God's desirous affecting humans, and *it`aruta de-le-tata* ("awakening from below"), viz., humans desirous affecting God. See *Zohar*: Va-yetse, 1:149a re Gen. 28:12; Va-yehi, 1:244b re Cant. 8:6, 1:245a re Prov. 10:25; Tazri`a, 3:45a–b re Deut. 4:4.

125. See B. Shabbat 105b; B. Yoma 23a re Judges 5:31; and B. Nedarim 22a–b and the scriptural citations there. Maimonides goes so far as to say that a leader who needs to intimidate his community (*le-hatil eimah*) should only feign feeling angry

outwardly while actually remaining unperturbed inwardly (*beino le-vein atsmo*), thus separating his external action from his internal state of mind (MT: Deot, 2.3).

126. Eliot, "Murder in the Cathedral," 221.

127. Heschel, *The Prophets*, 282–83.

128. M. Sanhedrin 6.2 re Josh. 7:19–25. There this is offered to those who have been convicted of a capital crime before their execution (MT: Teshuvah, 1.1 re Num. 5:6). Subsequently the formula "May my death be atonement (*kapparah*) for all my iniquities" became something every person who is aware of their very imminent death should say (B. Shabbat 32a). The assumption here is that we are all sinners whether originally or inevitably even if never convicted of a crime (let alone a capital crime like murder) in a human court (B. Shabbat 55a–b re Ezek. 18:20).

129. See B. Moed Katan 28b thercon.

130. The Greek verb *sympathein*, meaning to "feel-with," is like *Mitgefühl* in German.

131. B. Taanit 2a re Deut. 11:13.

132. B. Berakhot 7a. All "blessings" (*berakhot*) begin with the words "Blessed are You (*barukh attah*) Lord our God" before acknowledging what God has done in general or thanking God for what God has done for us particularly, or thanking God for specifically commanding us what to do (MT: Berakhot, 1.3–4). The *berakhah* here that God requests from Rabbi Ishmael is a human request for God to do something good for us. That God desires our prayerful requests, see B. Yevamot 64a.

133. Quoted in *Otsar ha-Geonim*: Berakhot, no. 28 re Exod. 34:6, ed. B. M. Lewin, 14–15.

134. Heschel, *The Prophets*, 269–78.

135. B. Shabbat 133b. This suggests that humans being made in God's "likeness" (*be-demut elohim*—Gen. 5:1) does not means that humans are like God ontologically but that humans are to act like God practically, that is, by imitating those divine actions God has revealed to humans, which are to be imitated by us.

136. B. Baba Kama 100a re Exod. 18:20; Baba Metsia 83a re Prov. 2:20.

137. B. Sanhedrin 6b–7a re Zech. 8:16.

138. *Vayiqra Rabbah* 4.6 re Jer. 50:17, ed. Margulies, 1:91–92; also, B. Berakhot 47b.

139. Text from *The Koren Mahzor*, 1475.

140. W. H. Auden, "September 1, 1939," in *Seven Centuries of Verse: English and American*, ed. A. J. M. Smith (New York: Scribner's, 1957), 687.

Chapter 4

Seeing God

Desiring Vision of God

In the covenantal relationship between God and the people Israel, all of the people are required to heed God's commandments (*mitsvot*). "Israel, do hear [*shema*]: the Lord is your God, the Lord alone" (Deuteronomy 6:4). The commandments are readily accessible to all the people to hear them and to do them. The Torah is not in heaven and far away from us. The Torah has been written down and carefully preserved. The Torah is now on earth (though not from the earth); "the word (*ha-davar*) is very close to us so that we can hear it in order to do it" (Deuteronomy 30:12, 14).[1] Nevertheless, what about seeing God or even trying to see God? Isn't that the desire of those who want the certitude of sight for most directly knowing the God with whom all of us are so related by hearing his commandments?[2] "My God, You do I seek [*ashahareka*]. . . . In the sanctuary I look for You [*hazitikha*] to see [*lir'ot*] Your power and Your glory!" (Psalms 63:2–3). Although we can understand or comprehend propositions that are themselves inherently invisible, we can only know or apprehend persons or even things that we can see or directly experience.[3] Knowledge (*da'at*) being immediate is greater than understanding (*binah*) that is mediated by ratiocination. As the great poet-theologian Judah Halevi put it about the Jerusalem Temple, "Happy is the eye that saw (*ra'ah*) it, to our regret our ear can only hear (*le-mishm'a*) of it."[4]

The question is whether seeing God or trying to see God is obligatory (*hovah*) for all of us like the obligation to hear God, or is it permitted (*muttar*) to some of us who desire this ultimate vision, or is it prohibited (*asur*) to all of us?

IS GOD TO BE SEEN?

The apparent meaning of three verses in the Pentateuch is that seeing God is an essential component of the obligation of every Israelite man to go up to Jerusalem as a pilgrim in order to celebrate in the Temple (*bet ha-miqdash*) there the three seasonal festivals: Passover in spring, Shavuot in summer, and Sukkot in autumn. "On three occasions during the year, every one of your males shall see [*yir'eh*] the face [*et pnei*] of the Lord God of Israel" (Exodus 34:23). The prefix *et* indicates that God is to be the direct object of the pilgrim's vision.[5]

Nevertheless, doesn't this contradict God's answer to Moses when he asked to see God: "You cannot see My face (*lir'ot et panei*) because no human sees Me (*yir'ani*) and lives" (Exodus 33:20)? How can an ordinary Israelite see, in fact be commanded to see, what Moses the greatest prophet could not see or was not allowed to see? Seeing God seems to be so overwhelming as to be fatal, hence wouldn't that vision inevitably kill any human who even tries to do so? Isn't that like what the people told Moses at Mount Sinai about the peril of hearing God speak with them directly: "You speak with us and we will hear it, but let not God speak with us lest we die" (Exodus 20:16)? And doesn't the Torah state later, "You should be very careful with your lives, for you didn't see (*l'o re'item*) any figure (*temunah*) on the day the Lord spoke at Horeb from the midst of fire" (Deuteronomy 4:15)? How can the Torah command ordinary humans to do what Moses couldn't do and survive? In fact, when it says that Moses "knew the Lord face to face (*panim el panim*; Deuteronomy 34:10)," a medieval exegete resolves the obvious contradiction with God's telling Moses he cannot see God by reading the text to be saying "God knew him (*yeda'o*) face to face, but Moses didn't know God face to face."[6] In other words, God saw Moses in a way Moses couldn't see God. The most Moses saw of God, according to the Talmud, was "through a shining mirror (*b'aspaqlaria ha-me'irah*)" while what the rest of the prophets saw of God was only through a cloudy mirror.[7]

Now if that is so, the apparent commandment to see God has to be interpreted in a way that doesn't take God to be the object of human vision. That, in fact, was done by rabbinic exegesis so that "all your males shall see (*yir'eh*) the face of the Lord" is now vocalized to read "every one of all your males shall be seen (*yeira'eh*) before (*el pnei*) the Lord" (as in Exodus 23:17).[8] Like Moses, every Israelite pilgrim doesn't see God but comes to be seen by God at the Temple in Jerusalem, where he has been commanded to present himself for God's inspection. The pilgrim is the object of God's vision at the particular place he has been commanded to present himself to be seen. But God is not visible at this particular place—or at any place in this world for that matter.

However, this revocalization is quite awkward syntactically, and the simpler reading of the verb "see" is not rejected entirely by this exegetical move. Instead it is reassigned. Thus a midrash states that "the way one would come to see (*lir'ot*), so one comes to be seen (*leira'ot*)."[9] This "would see"—that is, if one could see—seems to mean that even though God cannot be seen by any human eye, the pilgrims *would like to see God* nonetheless. Indeed, another rabbinic text states that "whoever fulfills the commandment to be seen it as if (*k'ilu*) he greets (*maqbil*) the divine Presence (*pnei shekhinah*)."[10] In other words, desiring to see God has not been denied but only sublimated. Along these lines, Maimonides interprets *seeing-and-being-seen* as follows: "Just as they come to be seen before God, so do they come to see His holy beauty [which is] the house of His Presence (*u-vet shekhinato*)."[11] Now there seems to be no prohibition of the desire to see God only the message that this desire cannot be fulfilled when one presents himself at the Temple for the celebration of the three pilgrimage festivals (*regalim*).

Another midrash states that the requirement of having the ability to see where one is commanded to be seen exempts the blind from the obligation to present themselves to be seen at the Temple in Jerusalem during the three pilgrimage festivals.[12] Therefore, while nobody is commanded to see God because God cannot or may not be seen, only those Israelites who are not blind have the obligation to *be seen*. It doesn't seem, however, that blind persons are actually prohibited from making the pilgrimage to be seen in the Temple. It is only that they are not fulfilling a literal commandment to do so. Instead they are performing a meritorious deed.[13] Surely obligating blind persons to do that would be placing an undue burden on most of them by making them undergo a journey that is taxing even on those who are not so handicapped. So just as God doesn't require the blind to see what they cannot see, so God doesn't require mortal humans to even try to see God, which they too cannot do or may not do.

GOD'S VISIBILITY

The questions now are (1) Is God invisible because embodied humans *cannot* see God due to the naturally limited capacity of humans? or (2) Is God essentially invisible to anybody due to God's immaterial nature? or (3) Does God not allow humans to see what God chooses not to be seen?

The view that God's invisibility is due to a human limitation comes out in a story told in the Talmud: Caesar said to Rabbi Joshua ben Hananiah, "I want to see your god." When Rabbi Joshua responded that he couldn't see him, Caesar persisted in his request, making it a demand. So Rabbi Joshua had Caesar face the sun on a bright summer day, telling the emperor, "Gaze (*istakel*) upon it." When the emperor told Rabbi Joshua, "I can't," Rabbi Joshua retorted, "If you can't gaze upon one of the creatures serving before God, all the more so can you not gaze upon the divine Presence (*shekhinah*)!"[14]

Now whether this encounter actually took place or not doesn't diminish the power of the theological point it makes as a parable. Moreover, the choice of Caesar in the parable is significant for two reasons. One, living in the second century, Rabbi Joshua was a subject of Roman imperialism in Palestine in late antiquity. Aware of this political fact, Rashi notes (in his comments on this Talmud text) that Caesar was not asking the rabbi to show him his (Jewish) god; rather, Caesar was ordering him to do so, like it or not. Two, some of the Roman emperors regarded themselves or were regarded by their subjects as gods. As such, they believed they had a supernatural power and authority that enabled them to see a fellow god.

The problem this parable poses is not with God's essential invisibility. Rather, the problem is with the essentially limited visual capacity of humans even regarding their vision of certain creatures let alone regarding vision of the Creator himself. Nevertheless, if the problem is with an inherent aspect of mundane human nature, couldn't God as the Creator of all nature (both human and nonhuman) change aspects of created human nature, that is, if God chose to do so? In other words, couldn't God choose to recreate human nature in another world? That would imply, though, that it is not that God is inherently invisible, it is just that mortal human creatures do not have the capacity to see what is beyond their limited visual range, that is, in this world.[15]

That humans cannot see God because God is essentially invisible has as its most prominent proponent Maimonides. In his commentary on the Mishnah, specifically in the tenth chapter of Sanhedrin (*ḥeleq*), which is the most theologically significant chapter in the Mishnah and the two Talmuds, Maimonides lists and explicates what he thinks are the thirteen basic principles (*yesodot*) that underlie the entire Torah and tradition. The third principle indicates about God that "you didn't see any picture (*temunah*; Deuteronomy 4:15)," which is to say one "couldn't apprehend (*hisagtem*) Him as depicted (*ba'al temunah*) because He is not a body or a force in a body."[16]

In a later work, Maimonides writes that "seeing" literally means "the sight of the eye" but it is "used figuratively to denote the grasp of the intellect." As such, "every mention of seeing, when referring to God . . . has this figurative meaning—as when Scripture says . . . 'I beseech Thee, let me see Thy Glory' (Exodus 33:18). . . . All this refers to intellectual apprehension, and in no way to the eye's seeing, as the eye can only apprehend a body."[17] One wonders, though, why Maimonides selected this verse (among others that speak of seeing God), which seems to be Moses's request to literally see or behold Godself. Whereas the usual interpretation is that Moses requested a bodily depiction of Godself visible to his eye (which God denies him), Maimonides holds that God denied Moses even intellectual apprehension of Godself.[18]

For Maimonides, God cannot be apprehended even by human minds let alone by human eyes because "this apprehension (*z'ot ha-hasagah*) is hidden and inaccessible in its very nature (*be-tiv'ah*)."[19] The term "nature" here seems to refer to both God's nature and to human nature. "Nature" means one's essentiality, constituting what one cannot be without. (Although Maimonides claims God's essence is unknowable, nevertheless we do know *via negativa* what does not essentially pertain to God's Being, thus clearing a path to ultimately know Godself positively.[20]) So if it is God's nature not to be a visible body, God is necessarily invisible.

Human nature, conversely, is to be incarnate in a finite body, hence humans are both visible and have the capacity for vision, both of which are proportionate to our finite bodies. As such, we humans are only able to see other finite bodies like ourselves. We cannot see what itself cannot be seen. For Maimonides, humans cannot choose to have an unnatural capacity to see what God himself has creatively willed not to be seen by any mortal, embodied creature. God remains in God's nature and humans remain in their nature necessarily. Humans who do pursue what could only be deemed an unnatural desire do so at their own peril. There is mortal danger (either death or insanity) when humans try to override their natural limitations.[21] Being perfect, however, God could have no such desire for what God already has by God's own nature, namely, God's self-knowledge.[22]

GOD'S FREEDOM

We have heretofore been dealing with necessary human nature and necessary divine nature. However, whereas our freedom of choice is circumscribed by our nature, God has the freedom to override his nature, his perfect, self-satisfied enclosure, if and when God so chooses to do so.[23] "Our God is in heaven, whatever He desires to do [*hafets*] God does" (Psalms 115:2).[24] As such, while humans in their present natural state cannot choose to see God, God can certainly choose to let humans see him. That, however, would mean that God has changed human nature in a world other than the present world (*ha'olam ha-zeh*). In fact, couldn't one very well say that the reason humans cannot see God in this world is because God has not let us humans do so? That disallowance could well mean that seeing God is prohibited by God. As such, anybody who claims to have seen God has violated what seems to be an implicit prohibition. In this view, it is not that even Moses *could not* see God; rather, it is that even Moses *ought not* see God.

This difference of interpretation comes out in how one translates Exodus 33:20. It is usually translated as "You cannot (*lo tukhal*) see My Face." This is a statement of fact. However, it could be translated as "You *may not* see My Face." That is a prohibition. Thus Rashi in his Torah commentary paraphrases this statement as "I don't give you permission (*noten lekha reshut*) to see My Face."[25] What isn't permitted is prohibited. Much earlier, Rabbi Joshua ben Korhah speculated that when Moses beseeched God, "Show me Your Glory" (Exodus 33:18), God said to him, "When I wanted to show you My face (*ke-she-ratsiti*) at the Burning Bush (Exodus 3:6), you didn't want (*lo ratsita*) to see My face; now that you want to see My face, I didn't want to show it to you."[26] As such, God's will trumps the will of any human, even the will of Moses. When God chooses that a human not see Godself, then no human should see or even try to see Godself.

Furthermore, if any human claims to see what no human ought to have seen, couldn't one infer that this presumptuous human has committed a transgression? This could be inferred from the second half of Exodus 33:20: "No human who sees Me lives (*ve-hai*), which could be translated "No human who sees Me *shall live*."

All this comes out in a vivid scenario in the Talmud when wicked King Manasseh executes the prophet Isaiah, charging the prophet, "Moses your master (*rabbekha*) said 'that nobody who sees Me [God] *shall live*'; but you said, 'I saw (*v'er'eh*) the Lord sitting on an high and exalted throne' (Isaiah 6:1)."[27] Elsewhere in the Talmud, it is mentioned that Manasseh made presumptuous interpretations of scripture.[28] Employing this kind of perverted exegesis, he convicted Isaiah of the crime of blasphemy, which is a speech-act for which a speaker deserves to be executed.[29] Notice that Manasseh doesn't accuse Isaiah of lying, that is, claiming to have seen what couldn't be seen by anybody or what couldn't be seen by himself as a prophet inferior to Moses. Rather, Manasseh accuses Isaiah of seeing and reporting to have seen what no human *ought* to have seen at all. In fact, if Isaiah had not reported what he saw, how would a human court convict this prophet for a private experience he'd kept secret? "Humans see appearances; only the Lord sees the heart" (I Samuel 16:7).[30] In defense of Isaiah, the Talmud concludes that what he saw was inferior to what Moses saw and that Moses only saw a better reflection of God than did any of the other prophets (Isaiah included), yet that reflection was not the prohibited vision of Godself.

We have seen now three different versions of why even the most exalted humans do not see Godself.

The first version asserts that Godself cannot be seen due to the nature of the object of vision. As such, no change in the nature of the human subject of vision could make visible what is necessarily invisible. This is a metaphysical explanation of why humans have not, do not, and will not ever see Godself. God is necessarily invisible.

The second version asserts that the problem is not with the object of vision but with the subject of vision, namely, the limited visual capacity of humans. As such, a radical change in human nature could enable such recreated humans to see what they previously could not see. This is an epistemological explanation of why humans have not and do not see Godself. There is nothing, however, to preclude the possibility that they will have the ability to see God if there would be a radical change in their bodily state bringing with it an immense improvement of their visual capacity.

The third version asserts that God is not necessarily invisible and that humans are not necessarily incapable of seeing God. Rather, it is that God has not chosen to let Godself be seen by humans. However, God could easily change his mind and willingly let Godself be seen by humans. From the human side of the relationship between God and humans, this means that God would allow at least some humans to see what had previously not been revealed to any of them. The implication here is that humans who willingly try here and now to see Godself are breaching a limit that God does not permit them to breach. This is a moral explanation of why even attempting to see God, although not proscribed in the Torah, seems to be a violation of a general prohibition of doing what no human has explicitly been permitted to do. As such, God's reply to Moses "Nobody who sees Me lives (*ve-ḥai*)" might be a warning that no human should even try to see Godself because it is mortally dangerous. In fact, there is a general prohibition of exposing oneself to mortal danger even for the noblest ends.[31] However, this might not be the case in a world radically different from this world.

These two points are expressed in the following midrash speaking of why the number of Levites diminished when Moses took the first census of the Israelites in the Wilderness in the second year after the Exodus from Egypt.

Why did the number of Levites diminish? It was because they had been seeing (*she-ro'in*) the face of the divine Presence (*pnei ha-shekhinah*) too much. . . . God said this happened in this world because they had been seeing Myself (*kevodi*), thus they perished (*hayu khalin*) as it says, "no man will see Me and live." But in the far-off future (*l'atid la-vo*) they will see Me and live forever. . . . Moreover, Me they will point out (*she-mar'in*) with their finger as it says (Psalms 48:15) "for this God is our God forever (*olam va'ed*); He will lead us beyond death (*al-mut*)."[32]

Note that the midrash says the Levites saw God, hence it was neither impossible because of God's invisibility nor because of the natural limits of the visual capacity of humans. Rather, the plight of the Levites was because they had violated what seems to have been a divine proscription of not only trying to see God but of actually seeing or viewing God. So in this view anyway, what the Levites did was possible. There was no impediment of what they were able to do either because of God's invisibility or because of the limited visual capacity of humans.

Along these same lines, another midrash states that while seeing God in the present world (*b`olam ha-zeh*) is impossible, in the far-off future, at the time of the "awakening of the dead" (*ha-qatsat ha-metim*), we will see God's likeness.[33] Indeed, this calls to mind Job proclaiming, "I know my Redeemer lives, even though He be the last to arise on earth, and after this is impressed in my flesh, I shall then behold (*ehezeh*) God" (Job 19:25–26).[34] One of the implications of the doctrine of the resurrection of the dead (*tehiyyat ha-metim*) is that despite losing their mortality, resurrected human bodies will still retain their bodily senses and especially their sense of sight.[35] The impossibility (*iy efshar*) of seeing God in the present world stated in this midrash is not a natural human impossibility.[36] Instead, it is a moral proscription. That is, God will not allow it to be done in this present world with impunity. As such, there is no way this voluntary human action can be justified.[37]

In this theological view, it will be God's choice (not God's necessity) that those he will resurrect in the world-yet-to-come (*olam ha-ba*) will see Godself. God will then fulfill this most sublime human desire.[38] The desire itself is necessary, that is, endemic, to human nature. What is voluntary, however, is how humans choose to act upon this desire. Therefore, the question is: Why does God deny the legitimacy of this necessary or natural human desire in this world when God promises to fulfill it elsewhere? Why is it that when humans choose to act on their desire to see God in this world, their choice is illegitimate, yet when they have their desire to see God graciously fulfilled by God in the world-yet-to-come, it will be meritorious? In fact, this will be their reward from God for repressing this very desire in the present world.

Furthermore, the midrash just quoted speculates that at the time of the resurrection of the dead, those whose bodily lives will have been restored to them will see God's face. Nevertheless, this midrash does not speculate as to what they will actually see. The scriptural proof-text this midrash bases itself on states, "I shall truly see (*be-tsedeq ehezeh*) Your face" (Psalms 17:15). Now in his commentary on Psalms, Rashi boldly paraphrases this text "I shall be satisfied (*esba`ah*) seeing Your picture [*temunatekha*] of Your likeness [*be-demut*] as it is said, "in the image of God [*be-tselem elohim*] did He make humankind [*ha'adam*]" (Genesis 9:6). So what Rashi is in fact saying is that those humans to be resurrected by God will actually see the source of their own reflection of God's face. In other words, they will see God truly as God sees them.

Perhaps this extraordinary comment of Rashi inspired Franz Rosenzweig to write the following about this sublime vision.

> In the innermost sanctuary of divine truth [*Wahrheit*] where he would expect that all the world and he himself would have to be relegated to the metaphor [*Gleichnis*] for that which he will behold [*erblicken*] there, man beholds nothing other than a countenance like his own [*Antlitz gleich dem eigenen*].[39]

SEEING AND HEARING

We need now to discern the difference between what seeing God in this present world involves and what might differentiate what might be called "mundane seeing" from seeing God in the world-yet-to-come. But first we must differentiate between seeing God's face and hearing God's voice. Our eyes and our ears seem to be the two sense organs with which we humans relate to God. It is only after this sensuous contact that our minds are able to understand the truth revealed in these sensuous experiences.

In scripture, hearing (*shmo'a*) is not primarily passively listening to someone else's voice then appropriating it for one's own enjoyment as when we listen to somebody singing. For example, "Let me hear (*hashmi'eni*) your voice, for your voice is sweet (*arev*; Song of Songs 2:14)."[40] Instead, hearing is primarily heeding God's commanding voice by doing what we have been commanded by God to do. We are thus dependent on the one we actively hear speaking to us. "If you surely hear My voice [*qoli*] by keeping My covenant" (Exodus 19:5).[41] "Does the Lord want burnt-offerings and sacrifices more than listening [*ki-shmo'a*] the voice of the Lord; behold, listening is better than sacrifice" (I Samuel 15:22).[42]

Even God's willingness to hear our voices when we supplicate him thereby makes God as it were dependent on us insofar as God thereby chooses to be affected by us. "Lord, hear my voice [*qoli*] when I call; be gracious to me and answer me" (Psalms 27:7). Nevertheless, the difference between our dependency on God and God's dependency on us is that God's dependency is itself voluntary whereas ours is involuntary. Our choice is not whether to be dependent or independent of God; rather our choice is only *how* we actively affirm or deny our dependency on God. This dependency itself can neither be created by us nor be obliterated by us. Conversely, God is free whether to be responsive to us or not. It is God's choice alone whether to be affected by us at all. Moreover, it is God's choice whether to respond or not respond to any of our particular requests upon him. So on the one hand, "Thus says the Lord God of Israel: I have heard [*sham'ati*] what you prayed to Me for" (II Kings 19:20). On the other hand, though, "Even when you pray very much, I do not hear it [*shome'a*]" (Isaiah 1:15).

Seeing, on the other hand, means one's taking an object into one's own visual range, framing it, and thereby taking possession of it. For example, "You will see [*ve-ra'ita*] among the captives a beautiful woman, and you will desire her, and you will take her as a wife" (Deuteronomy 21:11).[43] That is why seeing God or even trying to see God seems to be the arrogant attempt of creatures to define their Creator by enclosing him within the boundaries of their own experience. It would be altogether different, though, if seeing God were an all-consuming experience insofar as we would remain face-to-face with Godself and yet be unable to appropriate this encounter by taking it into our own separate domain.[44] This would be when God who always sees us finally lets us see Godself. Wouldn't that provide us with the certitude of direct contact with God yet without our taking that vision away with us as an enclosed, finite memory to be used by us whenever we might want to appropriate it? That, however, is not for us mortals in this present world. Here all-consuming contact with God is impossible because of other necessary relations of ours, both with other persons and things. These others themselves are not-God. They are only fellow creatures of God most of whom do not desire to see God as the seekers of Godself do.

This would only be possible in the world-yet-to-come (*ha'olam ha-ba*).[45] In that transcendent realm, as it is predicted in the Talmud, there will be "no eating, no drinking, no sex, no business dealings, no envy, no hatred, no rivalry. There the righteous (*tsaddikim*) will sit with crowns on their heads, enjoying the splendor of God's Presence (*ziv ha-shekhinah*)."[46] Now the scriptural proof-text brought for this assertion is "They beheld (*va-yehezu*) God while they were eating and drinking" (Exodus 24:11). The problem, though, with this text is that it seems to be plainly (*peshuto*) saying that the leaders (*atsilei*) of the people actually saw God in this world and that they did so while engaged in the mundane activity of eating and drinking. That is why the Talmud had to interpret their vision of God as a prediction of what will be possible for the righteous as their future reward in the world-yet-to-come. And Rashi interprets their eating and drinking metaphorically, namely, "They were satisfied by the splendor of the Shekhinah as if (*k'ilu*) they ate and drank."[47] In other words, the satisfaction humans would have with what would necessarily distract them from being involved with God in this world becomes symbolic of their total, undistracted satisfaction with totally seeing God in the world-yet-to-come.[48] There they will see God as God sees us in any world. And it is important to note that those resurrected by God for the world-yet-to-come will have their bodily sight restored to them. Yet their sight will have but one all-consuming object from whom their eyes will never wander, there being nothing else to distract them. "Whom else is there for me in heaven but You, and I desire no one else on earth" (Psalms 73:25).

That seeing God in the world-yet-to-come allows no distractions comes out in a poem by Judah Halevi when he longs for this sublime experience, saying,

> To meet the fountain of the life of truth I run, for I weary of a life of vanity and emptiness. To see [*li-r'ot*] the face of my King is mine only aim [*magamati levad*]; would that it were mine to see Him [*le-ḥazoto*] in a dream! Would I might behold [*eḥezeh*] His face within my heart! Mine eyes would never look beyond [*le-habit ḥutsah*].⁴⁹

This consummate experience will infinitely exceed the this-worldly experience of obediently heeding God's voice here and now. Nevertheless, even though heeding God's voice here and now doesn't guarantee that one will necessarily see Godself there and then, it seems impossible that anybody who didn't heed God's voice here and now would not be rewarded there and then with this sublime experience of seeing Godself. In another poem, Halevi says,

> My God, Your dwelling-places are lovely! It is in vision [*be-mar'eh*] and not in riddles [*be-ḥidot*] that my dream brought me to the sanctuary of God. . . . Then I woke, but You were still with me.⁵⁰

Judah Halevi was Franz Rosenzweig's great inspiration. At the conclusion of his masterwork *The Star of Redemption*, Rosenzweig like Halevi speaks of this consummate vision in the first person, which in no way could be described in the third person as if it were a mundane, objective experience.⁵¹ No doubt Halevi's words inspired Rosenzweig himself.

> God, who is the Last and the First, opened the doors of the sanctuary for me [*mir*]. . . . He let himself be seen [*Er liess sich schauen*]. He led me to that border of life where the sight is allowed [*verstattet ist*]. . . . That sanctuary wherein he allowed me [*mich*] to see had to be a piece of the supra-world [*Überwelt*]. . . . In the beyond [*jenseits*] of life . . . I see it, [*ich es schaue*], no longer merely hear.⁵²

NOTES

1. B. Baba Metsia 59b re Deut. 30:12.

2. For seeing as apprehension, see Maimonides, *Guide of the Perplexed*, 1.4.

3. MT: Yesodei ha-Torah, 1.10; also, Maimonides, *Shemonah Peraqim*, chap. 7, ed. Kafih, 260.

4. *Prayers for the Day of Atonement*, trans. D. de Sola Pool (New York: Union of Sephardic Congregations, 1967), 242. On the priority of seeing over hearing, note the great visual artist Leonardo da Vinci: "The eye, which is said to be the window of the soul, is the principle means by which the brain's sensory receptor may fully and magnificently contemplate the infinite works of nature. . . . Hearing is less noble than sight; as soon as it is born it dies, and its death is as swift as its birth. This does not apply to the sense of sight. . . . [What is seen] has great permanence." This quote is from Walter Isaacson, *Leonardo da Vinci* (New York: Simon & Schuster, 2017), 261–62.

5. This phrase is also found in Exod. 23:17 and Deut. 16:16. Only in Exod. 23:17 is the prefix *el* written rather than the prefix *et* that precedes the direct object of a verb. Nevertheless, even though *el* is in the dative case (see Lev. 1:1 and *Sifra*, par. 1 thereon), indicating an indirect object, its use in Exod. 23:17 seems to be accusative too. However, LXX makes it the indirect "before" (*enōpion/enantion*) as do the Targumim (*qadam*), that is, "before the Lord." See MT: Maaseh ha-Qorbanot, 4.11 re Lev. 1:9, 13; 2:2 (cf. B. Zevahim 46b). Note a more literal notion of seeing God on B. Menahot 43b re Num. 15:39.

6. Comment of Hezekiah ben Manoah known as Hizquni to Deut. 34:10, ed. Chavel, 607. This is consistent with the views of both Rashi and Rabbenu Tam on B. Hagigah 2a, *Tos.*, s.v. "yir'eh."

7. B. Yevamot 49b. See B. Sukkah 45b and B. Sanhedrin 97b re Ezek. 48:35. The word *ispaqlaria* is a hebraization of the Greek *speklarios* meaning "mirror" (Kohut, *Aruch ha-Shalem*, 1:191). The two types of mirrors mentioned on B. Yevamot 49b are discussed in M. Kelim 30.2; see Maimonides's comment thereon (ed. Kafih, 145; also, B. Rosh Hashanah 24a; MT: Qiddush ha-Hodesh, 2.5). For the difference between what Moses saw and what the other prophets saw, see *Vaqira Rabbah* 1.14 and the comments of Hai Gaon and Rabbenu Hananel quoted in *Otsar ha-Geonim*: Yevamot, ed. B. M. Lewin, 124–25, 314; also Nahmanides, *Hiddushei ha-Ramban*: B. Yevamot 49b re Job. 19:25. Cf. B. Megillah 19b and Rashi, s.v. "m'arah" re Exod. 33:22 and I Kings 19:9, where Elijah is the equal of Moses in what each of them saw of God.

8. LXX translates *yr'h* in all three verses with the passive *ophthēsetai*. The Targumim translate it with the passive *yithazun* or *yithamun*. Also see *Targum Onqelos* to I Sam. 1:22.

9. *Sifre*: Devarim, no, 143 re Deut. 16:16, ed. Finkelstein, 195–96; B. Hagigah 2a; also, B. Sanhedrin 4b and *Tos.*, s.v. "ke-derekh." Yair Hayyim Bachrach, *Responsa: Havvot Yair*, no. 203, cites *yir'eh/yeira'eh* as the strongest inner-textual biblical analogy (*heqesh*), being between two readings (*qri/qetiv*) of the same word. He notes B. Kiddushin 49b re Lev. 11:38 as another example of this kind of analogy.

10. Y. Hagigah 1.1/76a. For *maqbil*, literally meaning "causing to be accepted," as "greeting," see M. Avot 1.15.

11. MT: Hagigah 2.1. It is worth noting that the Samaritan version of Exod. 23:17 and 34:23 reads *aron* ("ark") rather than *adon* ("Lord") in the Masoretic text. See *Biblia Hebraica*, 7th ed., ed. Kittel (Stuttgart: Privilegierte Württ. Bibelanstalt, 1951), 114, 133. Also "before the Lord" (*lifnei Adonai*) as in Lev. 1:5 ("He shall slaughter the bull before the Lord") is not literally interpreted in the Talmud as "to

God's face" (*panim* as in Gen. 32:30) but rather as "within (*pnim*) the Temple precincts" (B. Zevahim 32b; B. Menahot 9a).

12. B. Hagigah 2a. See M. Nedarim 3.7.

13. See B. Kiddushin 31a and *Tos.*, s.v. "gadol."

14. B. Hullin 59b-60a and Rashi, s.v. "iva."

15. Note *Targum ha-Yerushalmi ha-Shalem*, ed. Rome to Exod. 33:20 (quoted in M. M. Kasher, *Torah Shlemah*, no. 129): "You are unable to see My face because it is impossible (*leyt efshar*) for any human to see Me and live."

16. *Commentary on the Mishnah*: Sanhedrin, chap. 10, intro., ed. Kafih, 142.

17. Maimonides, *Guide of the Perplexed*, 1.4, trans. S. Pines (Chicago: University of Chicago Press, 1963), 28.

18. Cf. Plato, *Republic*, 540A, who calls this kind of apprehension "lifting up the eye of the soul (*tēs psyches augēn*) to look up at what provides light to all and seeing (*idontas*) the Good itself." Like God for Maimonides, "the Good" (*t'agathon*) for Plato is the Absolute, beyond which there is nothing greater. Nevertheless, Plato claims for the soul's vision of the Good what Maimonides does not claim for intellectual apprehension of God.

19. Maimonides, *Guide of the Perplexed*, 1.21 (49).

20. See Maimonides, *Guide of the Perplexed*, 1.58; also D. Novak, *Law and Theology in Judaism* (New York: KTAV, 1976), 2:28–46.

21. T. Hagigah 2.3 re Ps. 116:15 and Prov. 25:16; Y. Hagigah 2.1/77b; B. Hagigah 14b re Ps. 116:15 and Rashi, s.v. "yaqar" re Exod. 33:20.

22. MT: Yesodei ha-Torah, 2.9–10; Maimonides, *Guide of the Perplexed*, 3.20–21.

23. Note E. LaB. Cherbonnier, "The Logic of Biblical Anthropomorphism," *Harvard Theological Review* 55 (1962): 192–93, 95: "The ineffable 'Ground of Being' is a God in chains. . . . Only if God is a definite, determinate personality can He take intelligible, purposive action. . . . The mystic's position is precarious. Suppose his God should one day want for himself the freedom to act and choose. . . . For the Bible to say that God is unlimited is simply to say that with God, all things are possible—even creation."

24. Note Franz Rosenzweig, *The Star of Redemption*, trans. B. E. Galli (Madison: University of Wisconsin Press, 2005), 24–25: "God has his nature, his essence by nature, his essence that is there [*daseindes Wesen*]. . . . This natural element in God alone gives him true autonomy [*Selbständigkeit*] in relation to all that is natural outside of him. . . . God is as little exhausted by the fact that God has a—his—nature. . . . God is not yet alive just from the fact he has how own nature. . . . Divine freedom must still be added."

25. For the need for authorization (*netilat reshut*) before doing something important, see B. Berakhot 28a and Y. Berakhot 2.8/5c.

26. B. Berakhot 7a and Rashi, s.v. "lo ratsitu" re Exod. 3:6. Following the comment of Abraham ibn Ezra on Exod. 33:18 (*kemo atsmekha*), the word *kevodekha* has been translated "Yourself."

27. B. Yevamot 49b. That God appeared in human form to the High Priest Simeon the Just when he entered the Inner Sanctum (*qodesh ha-qedoshim*) on Yom Kippur, see Y. Yoma 5.2/42a re Lev. 16:17. However, in the version of this story in Talmud

Bavli (B. Menahot 109b), the identification of "the old man," who appeared to Simeon the Just, with God is missing. See *Tos.*, s.v. "nizdamen lo" thereon.

28. B. Sanhedrin 99a re Num. 15:30.

29. M. Sanhedrin 7.5; B. Sanhedrin 56a.

30. See B. Kiddushin 49b.

31. See for example B. Avodah Zarah 12b; B. Hullin 10a; MT: Rotseah, 11.5.

32. *Tanhuma*: Bemidbar, 17 re Num. 3:15.

33. *Midrash Tehillim*, 17.3 re Ps. 17:15 and Isa. 26:19, ed. Buber, 134.

34. Note Thomas Aquinas, *Summa Theologiae*, 1, q. 12, a. 3 ad 1: "The words, 'In my flesh I shall see God my savior' (Job 19:26) do not mean that God will be seen with the eye of flesh, but that man existing in the flesh after the resurrection will see God" (London: Burns Oates & Washbourne, 1920), 126. Also note q. 12, a. 7 ad 1: "For he who attains to anyone is said to comprehend him when he attains to the words, 'I held him and I will not let him go' (Cant. 3:4)."

35. See *Beresheet Rabbah*, 14.3 re Gen. 2:7, and *Vayiqra Rabbah*, 14.9.

36. The doctrine of the bodily resurrection of the dead presupposes that for Pharisaic Judaism, a disembodied human existence, wherever it be located, is inconceivable. See B. Sanhedrin 91a–b; also Reinhold Niebuhr, *The Nature and Destiny of Man* (New York: Scribner's, 1943), 2:295–97, 311–12.

37. In his commentary *Or ha-Hayyim* to Exod. 33:20, Hayyim ibn Atar presents two views on this statement of the human inability to see God: (1) It is impossible even after death; (2) It will be possible after death, yet it still will not be quite what Moses asked God for.

38. For the futurity of these divine promises, see B. Berakhot 31a re Ps. 126:2; B. Sanhedrin 91b re Exod. 15:1; Josh. 8:30; I Kings 11:7. All of the biblical verses cited in these two Talmud texts begin with the word "then" (*az*) followed by a verb in the future tense. However, in biblical Hebrew, tenses are quite fluid. Thus "then" can be read as designating a verb in the past tense, for example, "then *did* Moses sing (*yashir*)" rather than "then *will* Moses sing."

39. Rosenzweig, *The Star of Redemption*, 446. On the other hand, Rosenzweig may have been thinking of Paul's very Jewish belief (cf. B. Yevamot 49b) that "Now (*arti*) we see (*blepomen*) through a glass darkly, but then (*tote*) face-to-face. Now I know partially, but then I will know as I am known (*kathōs epignōsthēn*)" (II Corinthians 13:12). Elliot R. Wolfson, *Through a Speculum That Shines* (Princeton, NJ: Princeton University Press, 1994), 325, notes that "the figural corporealization of God within the human imagination, is provided by Hosea 12:11." There God is reported to have said, "Through the prophets I let Myself be likened (*adammeh*)." Now Rashi gives two interpretations of this statement: (1) "I showed them many visions (*dummiyot*)." (2) God reveals Godself to the Prophets "through metaphors" (*al yedei meshalim*) in order to make their visions intelligible to their hearers (also see Ibn Ezra and David Kimhi thereto). Rashi's first interpretation seems to be a forerunner of the kabbalistic interpretation of the verse in *Zohar*: Bo, 2:42b.

40. For the sensual connotations of vocal music, see B. Berakhot 24a; Rabbenu Jonah (Gerondi) to *Alfasi*: Berakhot, s.v. "ervah," ed. Vilna, 17a.

41. See M. Berakhot 2.2 re Deut. 6:4 and 11:13 where *shmo`a* means accepting God's governance (*ol malkhut shamayim*) as authoritative and then accepting the specific commandments (*ol mitsvot*) as obligatory.

42. Let it be noted that the first sacrifice mentioned in scripture was by human initiative (Gen. 4:4) while the first mention of hearing (Gen. 3:8) is hearing the voice of God, accusing the first humans of violating the commandment from God which they had just heard (Gen. 2:16).

43. See B. Kiddushin 41a re Lev. 19:18. See also B. Baba Batra 2b and 60a re Num. 24:2 where looking at somebody else's property is considered a harmful, intrusive violation (*hezeq re'iah*) of one's neighbor's right to privacy. Along these lines, see T. Sotah 4.18–19; B. Sotah 9a–b. Also, deceiving somebody by performing an optical illusion is called "eye seizing" (*ha'ohez et ha`einayim*) discussed in B. Sanhedrin 65b; MT: Avodah Zarah, 11.9.

44. Note Y. Yoma 3.7/40d and B. Kiddushin 71a re Exod. 3:15 where it is taught that the Tetragrammaton was pronounced in the Temple by the high priest inaudibly so it could not be heard; hence it could not be appropriated by inappropriate persons (*pritsim*) for their own inappropriate use.

45. By translating *ha`olam ha-ba* temporally-eschatologically as "the world-yet-to-come" rather as "the eternal realm," I follow Abraham ben David of Posquières in his note (*Hasagat ha-Ra'avad*) on MT: Teshuvah, 8.8.

46. B. Berakhot 17a.

47. On B. Berakhot 17a, s.v. "va-y'okhlu." *Targum Onqelos* states that "eating and drinking" refers to their sacrifices being accepted favorably as if the leaders themselves had eaten and drunk them. However, *Tanhuma*: Beha`alotekha, no. 16 interprets their eating and drinking literally and thus judged to be impertinent, deserving of punishment later.

48. Isaiah ha-Levi Horovitz, *Shnei Luhot ha-Berit*, 2.3 (inyan ha`aqedah), interprets "as it is said today: on His mountain He will be seen (*yeira'eh*)" (Gen. 22:14), following Rashi's comment thereon that "today" (*ha-yom*) doesn't refer to the present, but to "future days" (*ha-yamin ha`atidim*). However, Rashi might only be referring to the time when the Temple will be built on this mountain, and when sacrifices will be offered there as Isaac was brought there to be sacrificed. Horovitz, though, takes *ha-yom* to refer to the eschatological future, citing "they shall see (*yir'u*) eye to eye the return of the Lord to Zion" (Isa. 52:8). See the comment of David Kimhi thereon; also, *Sifre*: Devarim, no. 352 re Gen. 22:14.

49. Jehudah Halevi, "Vision of God," in *Selected Poems of Jehudah Halevi*, ed. H. Brody, trans. Nina Salaman (Philadelphia: Jewish Publication Society of America, 1924), 115. Note that Halevi uses three different Hebrew verbs for "seeing," all having slightly different connotations. Now what Nina Salaman translated more literally as "mine only aim," Franz Rosenzweig *Jehudah Halevi: Zweiunneunzig Hymnen und Gedichte* (Berlin: Verlag Lambert Schneider, n.d.), 19, translated *was begehrt' ich noch* ("What more could I desire"). In fact, the title of the poem, "Were I to see His face" (*lu ehezeh panav*), which Salaman translated "Vision of God," Rosenzweig translated as *Sehnsucht* meaning "longing," but more literally meaning

"seeking sight." See Barbara Galli, *Franz Rosenzweig and Jehuda Halevi* (Montreal: McGill-Queens University Press, 1995).

50. Halevi, "My Dream," *Selected Poems of Jehudah Halevi*, 9.

51. When speaking of this experience, Rosenzweig uses the German term *Erlebnis*, meaning "inner-experience," rather than *Erfahrung*, meaning "objective" experience of things in the outer world. In this inner-experience, we encounter the unique, interpersonal events (*Ereignisse*) wherein God appears to us. See Rosenzweig, *Jehuda Halevi*, 30, where Rosenzweig speaks of "revelation" (*Offenbarung*) as being both *Erlebnis* and *Ereignis*.

52. Rosenzweig *The Star of Redemption*, 446. Let it be noted that for most of the rabbinic tradition, the experience of seeing God will be the reward of the righteous in the world-yet-to-come. Franz Rosenzweig, however, seems to be saying that he himself had this unique experience, this sublime vision, this epiphany, this revelation (*Offenbarung*, literally "disclosure") already in the past. From this overwhelming experience, he is then propelled into a life of hearing and doing the commandments at hand in the ordinary world. Hence the end of *The Star of Redemption* might very well be his own testimony. "The gate that leads out from [*herausführt*] the mysterious wonderful illumination [*Leuchten*] of the divine sanctuary where no man can remain alive " (447). In a comment on another poem of Halevi, Rosenzweig takes Halevi's statement of what *has already been experienced* (albeit in a dream) as forerunner of similar kabbalistic views (Rosenzweig, *Jehuda Halevi*, 173). See Wolfson, *Through a Speculum That Shines*, 14–24.

Chapter 5

Natural Law and Natural Theology
Two Approaches to Natural Law

The question of whether the idea of natural law can be accepted or must be rejected by the adherents of the three revelation-based, monotheistic traditions can neither be ignored nor dismissed out of hand. The question keeps cropping up regularly in the histories of Judaism, Christianity, and Islam, inevitably eliciting arguments pro and con.[1] For many years now I have been arguing that the idea of natural law has played a vital role in the development of the normative Jewish tradition. This is the tradition in which I am an active, committed participant at present and, it is hoped, into the future.[2]

We see this idea still playing a vital role both in the way the Jewish tradition is now to be interpreted internally and also in the way an authentic voice from the tradition can be brought into current, public, intercultural discourse on fundamental moral questions. The universal language and conceptuality of natural law seem to provide the most adequate medium for this discourse especially when the discourse is truly intercultural—that is, when natural law is neither used as a pretext for assimilating all others into one's own particular tradition nor projected as a universal ideal into which all particular traditions (including one's own) are to be assimilated.

Proponents of natural law (by whatever name it is called) in the Jewish tradition have generally employed one of two approaches. I shall argue for one approach as having greater heuristic value because of its greater correspondence with the Jewish tradition plus its having greater argumentative value for entering a coherent Jewish voice into current public discourse on the ubiquitous contemporary concern with universal human rights. To be sure the less-preferred approach has a venerable list of proponents whose views I shall try to depict fairly and respectfully before dealing with some problems this approach doesn't seem to be able to overcome. I shall then argue for the other, preferred approach. Nevertheless, what both of these approaches have in common is their opposition to the type of theological positivism, held by many Jewish thinkers, that rejects natural law altogether, regarding natural law as being incompatible with the normative Jewish tradition (and they have their Christian and Muslim counterparts).[3]

The first approach connects natural law and human goods. The second approach connects natural law and human rights. The first approach sees natural law as following from what has been called natural theology. The second approach sees natural law following from what might be called normative theology. Now the term "natural" minimally denotes what is distinct from "revealed." Thus natural theology is distinct from revealed theology (like what is told in scripture about God's interactions with humans); and natural law is distinct from revealed law (like the norms presented in scripture as God's explicit commandments to us humans).[4] For natural theology, natural law is rooted in a larger nature ruled by the Creator-God. For normative theology, the nature in natural law is human nature, which is essentially lawful, having been so made in his image by the lawgiving Creator-God.

NATURAL THEOLOGY: SAADIAH GAON

The first major rabbinic proponent of natural theology is the ninth-century philosophical theologian Saadiah Gaon, who I think still gives the best correlation of natural theology and natural law in the Jewish tradition. Saadiah connects natural theology with what he calls the "rational commandments" (*al-shariah al-aqaliah* in Arabic; *mitsvot sikhliyot* in Hebrew).[5] The concept of rational commandments seems to function quite similarly to the way natural law functions in the works of other natural theologians. Thus Saadiah writes,

> His [the Creator's] creation of all things was purely an act of bounty And grace. . . . Scripture says: "The Lord is good [*tov*] to all; and His tender mercies are over all His works" (Psalms 145:9). . . . He also endowed them [God's human creatures] with the means whereby they might attain complete happiness. . . . This means the commandments and the prohibitions God has commanded them.[6]

Now by "commandments" Saadiah means positive precepts or prescriptions ("Thou shalt"); by "prohibitions" he means negative precepts or proscriptions ("Thou shalt not").[7] Saadiah then asks why there are commandments at all since commandments seem to imply that God's creation needs obedient human action to be complete. Why didn't God simply make his humans creatures happy as their natural state of being? Instead of giving humans complete being, why did God put us in a state of becoming, impelling us to work for our own happiness as our practical goal? He answers these questions by making a commonsense point: humans appreciate the good they have attained by their own efforts more than any good that has simply been given to them even by God.[8] Conversely, the good or benefit given by God to all of his other creatures is in fact complete. Therefore, these other creatures do not need to be given the means towards an end that is already theirs at their creation. They don't have to work for what they already have. We humans, though, have to earn these good ends as the subsequent reward for our efforts because these good ends have not already been given to us at our creation. To humans alone does God give the means to choose what enables us to attain this good, this sought-after end for ourselves.

Furthermore, since Saadiah sees the primary human concern with God to be one of thankfulness for the gift of our existence, he thinks it is also obvious that we humans want to thank the one who has empowered us to become acting subjects having self-worth.[9] Conversely, it can be inferred from Saadiah's point about the rationality of thankfulness that we humans usually do not want to thank those who have overpowered us and reduced us to utter passivity. Indeed, we often resent such benefactors rather than thanking them since they have made us the objects of their largesse rather than the active subjects we humans want to be even if our benefactors did so benevolently.

As the means to the good ends their practice intends, the commandments (both positive and negative) could only be given to creatures who can choose whether to obey them or not. Moreover, since these commanded acts are of ultimate significance in the lives of their human recipients, the choice to keep them or not has serious consequences. The positive consequences of obeying the commandments are rewards; the negative consequences of disobeying them are punishments. Rewards are the good (*tov*) results to be sought; punishments are the bad (*ra*) results to be avoided.

The means to these evidently good rewards can be discovered readily through the exercise of our practical reason. As such, these acts do not really need to be commanded *to* humans at all (that is, heteronomously). In effect, they command themselves. They are what our practical or moral reason tells us we must do in order to attain our well-being in this world. They are the norms of which the Talmud notes, "if they hadn't been written down, reason [*din hu*] would have required they be written."[10] (This version of the idea of unwritten law seems to be akin to what the ancient Greek philosophers called *agraphos nomos*.[11]) Norms such as prohibitions of incest, murder, and robbery were only confirmed by scriptural revelation or the "Written Torah" (*torah she-bi-khtav*) even though they were already known and accepted beforehand from creation.[12] It was necessary that they be written down because the practical reasoning conducted in public discourse is constantly fluctuating, whereas writing these norms down authoritatively gives them immutability insofar as the Written Torah cannot be repealed or emended.[13]

The good ends intended by keeping the rational commandments are already known by humans from our ordinary interactions with other humans. But what are these good ends and why are the rational commandments the best means thereto? The answer is that insofar as humans are necessarily political beings, they need an ordered society to fulfill even their individual needs, all of which involve interactions with other humans. Only a society ordered by systemic law can fulfill the human need for rational order whose overall end is public harmony or peace (*shalom* in Hebrew). The commandments that comprise this law are themselves rational when they clearly function as the means intending this overall political end.

Along these lines, Saadiah argues that if stealing were not prohibited but instead permitted (with impunity), society would become undone because nobody would contribute to its economic development (which is necessary for its well-being). Taking somebody else's property would be easier than working to increase one's own property, yet that would not contribute to what has been called the common good (*bonum commune*). In fact, it would greatly detract from it.

The discovery of these well-known appropriate means to this overall good end does not require revelation. Therefore, these commandments are unlike the commandments called "revealed," which do require revelation.[14] That is because the supernatural ends to which these commandments are the means thereto are not known through our ordinary interactions in this world. When the ends are unknown, how could the means to them be known?[15] A road can only be plotted when its destination is known beforehand. Therefore, the means to these unknown ends must be given to us directly through revelation as commandments because we could never discover them by ourselves. These commandments, then, are not the stuff of natural law.

SIX QUESTIONABLE PROPOSITIONS
OF NATURAL THEOLOGY

We might see this grounding of natural law in natural theology expressed in the following six propositions.

1. The world, both its content and its structure, was created by God alone (*creatio ex nihilo*).
2. God has created the world in order to benefit his creatures.
3. All creatures are given their existence and are simultaneously given a distinct nature or essence according to which they are defined. A

creature's nature is how or the way God intends that creature is to behave appropriately or naturally in the world.

4. Human creatures are created according to their distinct nature but their nature is incomplete. As such, their being in the world is only their becoming what God has intended them to be. Toward this end, humans are only given the capacity or means by God, which are discoverable by human reason. Humans have to intelligently work in order to attain their complete their natural end. Understood as recompense for their efforts to attain them, these ends are the good states or situations humans work toward in order to enjoy them. These instrumental acts are neither ends in themselves, done for their own sake, nor are they done primarily because of their having been commanded by God. Humans want to do them primarily because of their evident results.

5. The end or good state that humans seek as naturally political beings is greater than the end or good state humans seek individually. That is because humans cannot attain their own individual rewards by themselves, outside their society.

6. Although these rational norms are also directly commanded by God in scripture, they are nonetheless already known by the exercise of unaided human reason devising the active means to these self-evident ends or good states. Historical revelation, then, only confirms the normative validity of these purposeful acts. Revelation does not institute them originally. In this view, imperatives are built into the good states God has enabled humans to attain by their own active means. As purpose-seeking beings, in their inescapable desire to enjoy these ends, humans learn from experience the appropriate means thereto. These good states are valuable because humans cannot help but want them.

Now all six of these natural theology and natural law propositions are highly problematic both in terms of what they propose regarding created nature and what they propose regarding the relation of theology and law in the Jewish tradition. They are problematic philosophically and theologically both in terms of their logic and in terms of how they correspond to the normative Jewish tradition. Let us now look at each one of them critically.

As to the first proposition, even though it is not irrational to believe that the natural world as we know it has been made by a cosmic Artificer, that doesn't tell us anything about the world that we wouldn't know without that belief.[16] In fact (at least, ever since Newton), we conceive of the world as operating equilaterally rather than hierarchically, that its entities function in a certain way by interacting with other entities correlatively rather than what is prior acting on what is posterior but not vice versa. Therefore, our explanation of the way the natural world operates doesn't require believing there is a first cosmic cause who like a human maker transcends what he or she has made both beforehand and afterward. Nor does it require us to believe that there has to be a master plan or architecture for the cosmos into which all natural entities are teleologically ordered, thereby assuming that the cosmos is finite by design.[17] Rather, in what might be called the modern paradigm, causes and effects are correlated: a cause is as dependent on its effect as much as an effect is dependent on its cause. In other words, nature cannot be constituted anymore as having a original efficient cause as its *archē* or *terminus a quo*, or as having an ultimate final cause as its *telos* or *terminus ad quem*.

Furthermore at the practical level, humans cannot discover by themselves the means to their ends in the cosmic hierarchy since such a teleological cosmology can no longer be affirmed.

Finally, as other advocates of natural theology have argued, affirming a first cosmic cause does not necessarily require one to acknowledge that this cause is *creator ex nihilo* (which the Jewish tradition certainly does affirm).[18]

As to the second proposition, here what is good is the benefit with which a person has been benefited by someone else. This benefactor is the external, greater cause of this benefit or gift that the giver of the gift has graciously given to the recipient of the gift. But how then do we evaluate what we have as being good and why do we have to believe it has been given to us by someone else rather than assuming that it has simply fallen into our possession? To answer these questions, we need to look at how we evaluate anything.

A person can evaluate some practice or some thing as being good because it is useful, that it is an effective instrument for achieving a state that is an end in itself. This is pragmatic evaluation. Or a person can evaluate some practice or some thing as "being good" because it is enjoyable per se, that it is valued for itself alone now and not as the means to something else later. This is hedonistic evaluation. Or a person can evaluate some practice or some thing as being good because it is beautiful, that it operates well by itself, independent of anyone's use or enjoyment of it. This is aesthetic evaluation (the Greek term *kalosk'agathos* is most apt here).

Nevertheless, this evaluative judgment, whether pragmatic or hedonistic or aesthetic, does not require us to attribute goodness to an external, higher cause. Finding something good in the world might only be fortuitous. Moreover, even if one believes that goodness has been caused by God as its first cause, this attribution doesn't entail the obligation to thank a cause with whom one is not already personally related.[19] Thankfulness can only be required for a gift explicitly given and explicitly received rather than for something discovered or found (like *nimtsa* in Hebrew) as simply being there (like *dasein* in German or *il y'a* in French). That is so even when one believes that what he or she has found was actually left there by an anonymous donor (like *es gibt* in German), whose very anonymity means this donor doesn't want to be thanked for their gift.[20] Conversely, the Torah is considered a good gift only when it has been lovingly received from its acknowledged Giver.[21]

As to the third proposition, it is true that all entities in the world have a nature, meaning they share certain essential traits common to their species. These common traits, by limiting what each one of them can and cannot do, also distinguish one species from another. Here again, one doesn't have to believe that God has specifically made them so. We could just as easily believe, in fact we could more easily believe (via Occam's razor), that their nature is immanent or inherent and not have to assume that it has been imposed upon them by a greater, external cause.

As to the fourth proposition, acts done for the sake of a reward are basically selfish, only involving others when these others are the means to one's own good. However, stealing is basically wrong because it violates the right of another person to their own property and not basically because of its bad effect on political order, which one only respects when it is in one's own immediate self-interest to do so. A bad effect on political order is a secondary result of an unjust act and not the chief reason (*ultima ratio*) why it ought not to be done.

As to the fifth proposition, it is true that humans seem to seek their own good (*bonum sibi*) as an end in itself. Yet we only seem to seek the general good of our own society as a means or an instrument for attaining our own special good. Even a thief could admit that the economy of any society would break down were everybody to steal from everybody else, thereby agreeing that their society is justified in forbidding all its members from stealing, and that it is justified in punishing anybody who does steal. Even thieves are in favor of this prohibition-then-penalty in general for were everybody to steal from everybody else with impunity, even thieves would have no societal protection of their own private property from other thieves.[22] Nevertheless, this particular thief is not everybody but thinks of himself or herself as somebody special who is a singular exception to the general rule.[23] Many thieves rationalize that their circumstances are unusual, pressuring them to steal in order to survive. Being an exception, though, means that the economy of their society will not break down when only a small minority of its members steal from one another or when an even smaller minority steal regularly. This notion of the common good, then, does not sufficiently undergird the universal prohibition of stealing. Following this view, one cannot say that the common good is greater than one's individual good.

As to the sixth proposition, it would seem that a law, whatever its source, is essentially a command (*mitsvah* in Hebrew). It is more than an ad hoc decree. It is part of a normative whole called the "Law" (*ha-torah* in Hebrew or *ho nomos* in Greek).[24] Nevertheless, at least in this kind of natural theology as it pertains to the interpersonal relations that are the subject of natural law, only those who have to be told what to do by a superior (heteronomy) need explicit commandments. More intelligent persons can figure this out by themselves for themselves. Hence, being commanded is secondary to rational discovery. Conversely, in the Jewish tradition, being commanded is primary, and the one and only authentic source of all commandments is God. As scripture puts it, "The end of the matter, when everything has been heard, is to be in awe [*yer'e*] of God and to keep His commandments, for that is all there is for humankind [*kol ha'adam*]" (Ecclesiastes 12:13). Since natural theology doesn't primarily conceive of God as the lawgiver, that fact causes Jewish opponents of natural theology–based natural law to argue that natural law is essentially foreign, indeed antithetical, to the authentic, normative Jewish tradition. That is the main theological objection to any Jewish version of natural law.

Therefore, in order to retain natural law as integral to the Jewish tradition, we need to constitute a different theology as its ground.

NORMATIVE THEOLOGY AND NATURAL LAW

Deriving natural law from natural theology seems to violate what has been called the "is-ought" distinction.[25] That is, to say that something *is* the case (like saying that God created the world or even saying that God created the world for a reason or purpose) doesn't logically entail that one *ought* to do anything at all therefore. The acknowledgment of this fact (from *factum* in Latin meaning "what has been done" or "deed") does not lead to any obligation to worship God, to obey God, or to hope for salvation from God. It brings no religious imperative ipso facto. That is the main philosophical objection to grounding moral law in natural theology.

From the problematic outlined above, one could conclude that if natural law stems from natural theology, and if natural theology is refuted, natural law then goes down with the ship. Nevertheless, one can assume that natural law would be better undergirded by a kind of theology other than natural theology. That better undergirding comes from what could be called "normative theology." It can provide a more direct connection to natural law than natural theology can by affirming the primacy of being-commanded, or what could be called "normativity." It is also closer to revealed theology than is natural theology even though it is not derived from special revelation. (Every Jewish theology, if it is to be traditionally Jewish, must show its closeness to revelation however it theorizes that proximity.)

Furthermore, because it is not derived special revelation, advocates of normative theology can adequately answer the charge that natural law, promoted as it is almost exclusively by believers in divine revelation, is really nothing but a covert rationalization of their revelation-based theology's particularism masquerading as universalism. Those who derive natural law directly from special revelation, however, cannot do this as they often reduce natural law to what their particular faith community wants to apply universally because of their own authority. That is why they are unable to answer very well the charge that natural law is the imperialistic project of their own particular traditional community to normatively colonize the rest of humankind.

Those who do not require natural law to have any ontological-theological undergirding have no answer to the charge that all law is positive law and that what is made by humans can just as easily be unmade by humans. This soon becomes the charge that natural law is but an imaginative human projection onto an otherwise indifferent universe.[26]

We have seen that natural law does not necessarily stem from natural theology. Anybody who asserts that it does stem from natural theology thereby commits the logical error of deriving prescription (ought) from fact (is), even from the most basic of all theological facts, that the universe has been made by God. The best way to overcome this impasse is to argue that the precepts or commandments of natural law are essentially the duties commanded to correlate with basic human rights, which are essentially oughts not facts. This is a philosophical task. Also, we have to argue that the prescriptions or precepts of natural law as divine law presuppose a prior fundamental prescription or commandment, which could only come from God. This is a theological task. Finally, we have to argue that the existence of the universe in which natural law is natural or endemic stems from God's creative commandment to all that exists: to be (its existence) *what* it cannot be otherwise (its essence or nature). In this way, it can be shown that it is not illogical to derive an is from an ought whereas it is illogical to derive an ought from an is. This is a metaphysical task. As Abraham Joshua Heschel put it so beautifully,

> Against the conception of the world as something just there, the Bible insists that the world is creation. Over all being stand the words: Let there be! . . . To be is to obey the commandment of creation. . . . Philosophically the primacy of creation over being means that the "ought" precedes the "is." The order of things goes back to an "order" of God.[27]

NATURAL LAW AND HUMAN RIGHTS

A human right is a justifiable or reasonable claim of any human on any other human. A human duty is an appropriate response to what the rights-holding person is properly asking that other person to do or not do. A duty logically presupposes a right that engendered it. It is what one owes (in Hebrew, *hov*, which is a "debt") the rights-holder claiming him or her.²⁸ In our temporal experience, though, we have to be claimed or duty-bound before we can cogently claim dutiful responses from others. We wouldn't know how to make a reasonable rights-claim unless we had been reasonably claimed by someone else previously.

When a claim is proper, the dutiful response so claimed is reasonable because the claim itself is reasonable. It is a justified request ipso facto. Law transforms such reasonable requests into commandments or precepts, that is, it translates claims originally uttered in the first person (I) into claims subsequently uttered in the third person (she or he or they). In other words, a right is originally a claim directly made by one person who bears that right to a second person (you) to dutifully respond accordingly. These duties are subsequently proclaimed by the Law indirectly on behalf of all bearers of this right. This universalization now legitimatizes the right, making it more than an individual, idiosyncratic plea. Natural law makes this universalization extend to all humans in any society on earth.

Commandments that pertain to human interactions not only must have reasons for why they are to be done willingly by reasonable persons, they also require an ultimate source or authorization. That is because in our significant human interactions, all of which involve claims having moral weight, we need to know *who* claims us rightfully or not then *what* we have been commanded to do by and for the one rightfully claiming us and then *how* or *the way* we are to fulfill the claim made upon us in accordance with the intention of the one so claiming us. Finally, we need to know *why* this claim is reasonable or not.

Now this enquiry, this looking backward, cannot go on forever. So to avoid an infinite regress, we need to suppose that God as Creator is the original rights-holder and that God cannot be conceived as being beholden or duty-bound to anyone greater than Godself since God is whom no one greater could be presumed to exist. (This logic is similar to the logic of natural theology, where it is assumed that God is the only cause who is not himself caused by anyone else.) However, when does a human person invoke God as the ultimate rights-holder, and how does that undergird natural law?

Scripture records the first normative contact between God and humans in these words "The Lord God commanded [*va-yitsav*] humans [*adam*]" (Genesis 2:16). This is the prime commandment (the German term *Grundnorm* is most apt.) The word "humans" (*adam*) is interpreted by the rabbis not as designating the person *to* whom the divine command is addressed (that is to be assumed and need not be said), but rather, it designates the person *of* whom the prohibition is meant to protect. So the verse is now meant to be read as "The Lord God commanded humans not to shed the blood [*shefikhut damim*] of [*'al*] other humans."²⁹ God is thereby proclaiming he doesn't want bloodshed in his world by prohibiting it. The earth is the habitat assigned to humans by God.[30] It is created for human dwelling (Isaiah 45:18); and it is cursed when human blood has been shed upon it.[31]

The first command addressed to the only creatures capable of being commanded by God is the prohibition of murder.[32] That explains why God judges Cain to be guilty of the murder of his brother Abel. It can be assumed Cain already knew its prohibition. But how does Cain know God has prohibited murder? Surely one cannot reasonably be held responsible and thus subject to punishment for an act that has not been prohibited.[33] But, from whom did Cain first hear this prohibition and that it pertains to all humans like himself?

Following this rabbinic version of the biblical narrative, Cain knew his duty was to respect the life of any other "child of Adam and Eve" (who are humankind) because his parents conveyed the commandment of God to him and to his brother. Being mediated through them, they had to say it in the third person: God prohibited it. However, since this duty is commanded because of the prior right of every human being not to be killed by any fellow human being, the commandment has more immediate personal force when the original right is uttered directly from the mouth of the bearer of this right-bearer to the ears of the bearers of the duty to do their duty to this person here and now.

The great rabbinic scholar Louis Ginzberg (d. 1953), paraphrasing several rabbinic texts, has Abel saying to Cain, "God, who brought us into the world, will avenge me."[34] Yet surely Abel couldn't say this unless his prime right or claim on Cain was that he not be killed. Indeed, it is the violation of this claim that God has prohibited in the law and that the violation of which will not go unpunished. Abel's claim is a demand that justice be done first by Cain not to kill him, then a demand that God not let Cain get away with his crime.[35] So it is reasonable to assume that Abel demanded of Cain as his right, "Don't kill me!" This is the right of a would-be victim (*nirdaf*) to utter to his pursuer (*rodef*) whom, in fact, he or she is allowed to kill first if the pursuer will not listen to this demand.[36] Nevertheless, this is not a plea for mercy, which would be an appeal to Cain's largesse, since a refusal to be merciful is not legally punishable.[37] Abel is demanding justice: that his right not be violated. This is like Abel's blood that had been shed by Cain now "crying [*tso`aqim*] to Me" (Genesis 4:10). This is not an appeal to God's mercy, that is, for God to save the victim (as it is too late for that). Instead, it is a demand that God do justly by avenging Abel's murder by his brother Cain.[38] One's right not to be killed is a prima facie claim on all others. How could anybody argue against it? That is, unless they themselves want to be killed, which most of us would regard as the unreasonable claim of a desperate person that nobody ought to comply with.

Who, however, is the source of the rights or claim of the victim on his victimizer? This question must be asked, ultimately if not immediately, because a right is an entitlement. So the question to be asked of the rights claimant is Who entitled you to make this claim? In whose name are you claiming my dutiful response? That is because we cannot entitle ourselves any more than we can command or create ourselves. "Entitle" (*zakkei* in Hebrew) like "command" (*tsavei* in Hebrew) is a transitive verb, whose subjects must intend objects different from themselves. As Thomas Jefferson put it so well in the *Declaration of Independence*, human rights are "unalienable" because all humans have been so "endowed by their Creator."[39] The entitlement or granting of a right (the most basic right being the right to life) is simultaneous with the commanding of the appropriate duty. The right entails the duty as the duty presupposes the right. So when God prohibits murder he thereby entitles murder victims with the right not to be murdered. And if they have been murdered, they have the right that their murder be avenged by God's judgment of their murderer.[40]

Furthermore, while some rights may be waived at the discretion of those to whom they have been given, the right to life may not be waived.[41] So when we desire to waive our right to life by committing suicide, remaining alive then becomes a duty we now have to uphold.[42] And when we are unable to perform this duty for ourselves, bystanders are obligated to do so on our behalf.[43] God's right to give and take one's life trumps any human right to contravene God's right by humans asserting a right of their own.[44]

Now this could well be the meaning of the biblical assertion (Genesis 1:26, 9:6) that humans are created "in God's image" (*be-tselem elohim*). God makes his claim on us humans not to murder our fellow humans who represent God image (*imago Dei*) by acting as the subjects of God's prohibition of murder, acting in relation to our fellow humans who represent God's image by being the objects of the prohibition of murder. As subjects, we thereby become the medium through which God's will is heard and obeyed. As the image of God, we become the objects of either respect for God or antagonism toward God. As the image of God whom God has cast into the world, a direct assault on us is ultimately an assault on God who created all humans as God's image, being God's representatives in the world. Thus Abel seems to be asking God to avenge Cain's assault on Godself, an assault committed on Abel's own body, which is the only site where this assault could be effective.[45] It could be said that God doesn't give rights to humans to do what contradicts God's purposeful, positive creation.[46]

We humans act as God's image by imitating or representing God as "God's likeness" (*be-demut elohim*).[47] We do this by making a rightful claim on one another. Therefore, God judges Cain for having violated God's commandment, meaning that God is exercising his primordial right *through* Abel's rightful claim on Cain not to kill him and *through* Abel's posthumous claim on God to judge Cain, his fellow human creature, for not doing his duty to respect Abel's right to life instead of violating it. This claim may be made on God, because as "the Judge of the whole earth" (Genesis 18:25), God has promised to rectify injustice on earth fairly—as later in the biblical narrative Abraham is invited by God to remind him (Genesis 18:17). As Rabbi Akivah taught, humans naturally sense somehow or other that we represent a higher authority and that in biblical revelation we are subsequently told just who that highest authority is and more of what God wants us to do in his name in the world.[48]

The minimal commandments of God are to be known and kept before God's full law is revealed. Therefore, it is correct to call these minimal commandments natural law because they pertain to universal human nature as the image of God in the world. Even though the texts in which we have seen accounts of the practice or violation of universally valid moral norms are from biblical revelation, these texts are not immediately prescriptive. Rather they recall the norms all humans are supposed to have known already and must be aware that they cannot be violated with impunity. In other words, these norms are prior not subsequent to specifically scriptural revelation of them.

Now direct scriptural revelation is the source of halakhah as Jewish positive law. So what is the connection between natural law and positive law in the Jewish tradition?

NATURAL LAW AND POSITIVE LAW

Natural law is universally valid insofar as it applies to all humans anywhere and everywhere. Nevertheless, all humans to whom natural law applies still have to live somewhere. That is, each of us has a specific address in this world (even when we wander away from it voluntarily or are exiled from it). The world at large, however, is nobody's address. We all live in specific polities, each having its own positive law. Each polity is its own jurisdiction.[49] (The German term *Rechtsstaat* is most apt here.) That jurisdiction applies only to members of (and to resident-aliens in) that distinct polity. Nobody lives by natural law alone. This is true of the scripturally based law Jews are required to live under. It too is positive law even though the giver of that specific law is the creator and ruler of the whole universe.

For those Jews who recognize only Torah law as valid for them, universal law is valid only for non-Jews. However, by precluding themselves from the law that is valid for Gentiles, Jews cannot claim its universality anymore since at most it is now a law for everyone else but the Jews. So when Jews promote the Noahide commandments as, in effect, Jewish law for Gentiles, their promotion becomes an imperialist project even when benignly presented. (It is like *ius gentium*, which was Roman law as it applied to Roman subjects who, unlike full Roman citizens, were not governed according to *ius civile*.[50]) On the other hand, for those Jews who recognize a truly universal law—which is natural as it pertains to universal human nature and which is valid for *all* humans, Jews included—what then is the connection between universal law and their own positive law to actually live by here and now and forever?

I would say that universal or natural law is the criterion by which it is ascertained whether positive Jewish law is consistent or inconsistent with human nature as the image of the just God. Therefore, if a positive law, even if scripturally mandated, appears to be unjust—that is, inconsistent with divinely made natural law—the authorized interpreters of positive Jewish law are morally obligated to overcome this inconsistency. "Justice, justice you shall pursue!" (Deuteronomy 16:20).[51] That is to be done even if it necessitates radical reinterpretation of the text of scripture. Indeed, without such reinterpretation, the law as literally interpreted and applied seems to tarnish God's just reputation.[52]

A most pertinent example of this kind of radical reinterpretation is how the biblical command to kill the Canaanite population in the land of Israel at the time of the conquest of the land under Joshua's leadership is so reinterpreted (even though it has been long inapplicable). Notwithstanding the fact that scripture states, "You shall no let anybody live" (Deuteronomy 20:16), there are good reasons to suppose that this commandment was never categorically carried out in Joshua's time and to suppose there are good reasons it couldn't be carried out after the destruction of the First Temple in 586 BCE. Moreover, the Jews at the time the rabbis were pondering this moral dilemma didn't have the power to do so anyway.[53] Despite the fact that this dilemma is theoretical, the rabbis were clearly troubled by the scriptural commandment nonetheless.

Doesn't the literal interpretation of this commandment mean the indiscriminate extermination of humans irrespective of whether they deserve punishment or not? Isn't this a violation of the basic human right to life that Abel invoked against his murderous brother Cain? Moreover, didn't Abraham question God's justice when God proposed the wholesale destruction of the cities of Sodom and Gomorrah? "Will the judge of the whole earth not act justly (*l'o ya'aseh mishpat*)?" (Genesis 18:25). How can humans imitate what seems to be God's irrational injustice? How can we imitate in our dealings with others (Genesis 18:17–19) what seems to be inimitable? How could this be the will of the God of whom Moses said, "All His ways are just (*mishpat*). . . . Right (*tsaddiq*) and straightforward (*yashar*) is He" (Deuteronomy 32:4)?

These are all cogent objections based on what are considered universal rights, namely, the right not to be killed indiscriminately and the right to a trial of each individual for his or her own misdeeds alone.[54] To answer these objections, rabbinic interpretation of this commandment took what seems to be a categorical imperative and made it into a hypothetical imperative. That is, what seems to be an unconditional, apodictic norm became via rabbinic exegesis quite conditional. This was done by surmising (or perhaps invoking a forgotten tradition) that before the invasion of the land, Joshua sent a letter to the entire Canaanite population offering them conditional peace terms that if accepted would not only spare them from being killed by the Israelites but would preserve their sovereignty as well.[55] In other words, by accepting reasonable peace terms, the Canaanites would lose neither their lives nor their liberty.

In his further development of this rabbinic reinterpretation of the biblical commandment, Maimonides added two significant points.[56] First, the Canaanites had to acknowledge Israelite sovereignty in the land of Israel. This was to be done by their paying tribute (*mas*) to the Israelite polity but of an unspecified amount (which suggests it was considered negotiable). It would seem that this acceptance on their part would preclude the Canaanites from being taken as slaves by the Israelite conquers. Second, the Canaanites had to accept the seven Noahide laws, which would be actually reacceptance of them because they are considered primordial.[57] The most evident of these commandments is the prohibition of shedding innocent human blood (*shefikhut damim*), which itself is a prohibition that the indiscriminate killing of a conquered population would most certainly violate. One cannot condemn in others what one has not first condemned in oneself.[58] Indeed, an important principle in the Talmud is that nothing originally prohibited to the Gentiles (including the Jews themselves before they entered the Sinaitic covenant) is subsequently permitted to the Jews.[59]

What this indicates about the relation of natural law and positive law in the Jewish tradition is not that natural law trumps positive law. Positive law always retains its prima facie authority. Rather, natural law becomes the criterion for the interpretation or reinterpretation of positive law. It is positive law's necessary presupposition (*conditio sine qua non*) but not its sufficient ground (*conditio per quam*) by which positive law could be annulled. So we now need to look for what natural law has in common with the two types of Jewish positive law.

All law in the Jewish tradition is ultimately if not immediately taken to be divine law.[60] Nevertheless, there is a difference between biblically derived (*d'oraita*) law and law rabbinically enacted (*de-rabbanan*). The latter is allowed to be enacted because of a general divine mandate for the Sanhedrin and its rabbinical successors to do so.[61] Distinct from both kinds of positive Jewish law is natural law that, as we have seen, is revealed through the voices of vulnerable humans claiming as their entitlement from God that their

lives, their bodies, and their property not be violated by other humans—and
that God enforce their rights both before and after they have been violated.
Human rights-holders also have a claim on their society to enforce their rights
in loco Dei as it were.⁶²

Furthermore, biblically derived law can never be repealed, at least in
this world.⁶³ Rabbinically enacted law, however, at least in principle can be
repealed.⁶⁴ As for natural law, being the normative content of the perpetual
Noahide covenant made by God, it too cannot be repealed by humans and, it
seems, it will not be repealed by God.⁶⁵ And like both biblically derived and
rabbinically enacted law, Noahide law as (arguably to be sure) the Jewish
version of natural law can be observed without an acknowledgment of its
divine source. Nevertheless, this theological acknowledgment will make the
Gentiles who make it equal to Jews in the kingdom of God in the world yet
to come (*ha`olam ha-ba*).⁶⁶ Only this explicit acknowledgment recognizes
what seem like wise counsels to be authentic divine imperatives (*mitsvot*).⁶⁷

NATURAL LAW AND ONTOLOGY

So far this exercise in normative theology has shown that the norms of
natural law are *oughts* grounded in the foundational *ought*. Unlike natural
theology examined earlier, we have avoided the fallacy of deriving oughts
from an *is*, or foundational fact. Nevertheless, it is not a fallacy to infer an
is or state of affairs from a prior *ought*. This is the case when we practice
justice effectively in the world because God has so commanded us to do so.
"The work [*ma`aseh*] of righteousness will be peace [*shalom*]; and the effect
[*v`avodat*] of righteousness will be tranquility and serenity" (Isaiah 32:17).
When humans do this, it is the result of an *ought* that God has commanded
authorizing or entitling humans to partly realize in the world.⁶⁸

This inference of a fact from a command—an *is* from an *ought*—is not
only the case in the human world, it is already the case in the creation of the
cosmos within which humankind emerges and endures. The cosmos is the
factual result of a primordial divine command. Hence humans need to know
what the created natural order is so as to be able to properly keep the commandments given by the Creator to be kept here.

Effecting justice is not only imitation of God as "the Judge [*ha-shofet*]
of all the earth" (Genesis 18:25), it is imitation of God as the creator of the
whole universe. Thus it is declared in the Talmud that "every judge who
effects a true judgment [*din emet*] truthfully, even for a moment, it is as if
he has been made God's partner (*shuttaf*) in the working (*be-ma`aseh*) of
creation."⁶⁹ That is because scripture states about creation, "For He spoke
and it came to be (*va-yehi*); He commanded (*tsivah*) and it endured" (Psalms

33:9). God created the cosmos by commanding it into existence justly. At the very beginning, God said, "Let there be (*yehi*) light, and light came to be (*va-yehi*)" (Genesis 1:3). Earthly justice is thus consistent with natural cosmic justice; it is not a cosmic fluke. The universe itself is normatively constituted. "The laws (*huqqot*) of the heavens" precede God's "rule on earth" (Job 38:33).[70] As such, humans can only be God's junior partners, can only imitate but can never emulate God. "To whom would you compare Me; to whom would you make me equal (*ve-tahsvu*); to whom would you liken Me so as to be similar [*ve-nidmeh*]?" (Isaiah 46:5).

All this needs to be emphasized since the normative theology advocated here has heretofore seemed to lack ontological grounding. But without it this theology only deals with the interpersonal human world apart from the wider cosmos in which it needs to be situated. That ontological grounding is only rational and not fantastic or bizarre when it is understood as being the cosmic background of the normative nature of human persons. Nevertheless, this is not a return to natural theology. Instead, it is a normative constitution of created nature. The difference is that theology as the commanding "word of God" (*dvar adonai*) is the source of all nature both human and nonhuman and not that the commandments of God are inferred from created nature. As such, affirming God's original authority over interpersonal relations in this world is more than a postulate of practical reason. Rather, that affirmation stems from God's cosmic authority primarily considered ontologically. "The Lord rules; the world [*tevel*] is firmly established [*af tikkōn*] and is not moved. . . . He comes to judge the earth and its peoples with faithfulness" (Psalms 96:10, 13).

Finally, natural law can only constitute the rights and duties that pertain to interpersonal human relations. It cannot constitute the rights and duties that pertain to the covenantal relationship between God and humans. That constitution can only come directly from the special revelation that scripture proclaims and whose special commandments it prescribes. That is why natural law is necessary but not sufficient for true human flourishing that not only comes from God originally but is more immediately lived with God. This covenantal relationship is one of love, which is an intimate mutuality going far deeper than the domain of law, justice, and rights.[71] Moreover, whereas in the domain of natural law God entitles humans to make claims or exercise our rights upon each other, in the covenantal realm God makes claims for Godself. Human claims upon each other are revealed generally in ordinary interpersonal relations. God's claims upon us for Godself are revealed in the special revelation proclaimed in scripture. All that notwithstanding, this deeper covenantal realm does not escape the domain of law, justice, and rights, which still is the anchor that keeps it attached to this human world here on earth.

NOTES

1. See Anver Emon, Matthew Levering, and David Novak, *Natural Law: A Jewish, Christian, and Islamic Trialogue* (Oxford: Oxford University Press, 2014).

2. My main discussions of natural law are found in David Novak, *Natural Law in Judaism* (Cambridge: Cambridge University Press, 1998); David Novak, *Covenantal Rights* (Princeton, NJ: Princeton University Press, 2000); David Novak, *The Image of the Non-Jew in Judaism*, 2nd ed. (Portland, OR: Littman Library, 2011); and David Novak, *Jewish Justice* (Waco, TX: Baylor University Press, 2017). A number of key points, originally made in these earlier works are developed in this chapter but most often without specific citation.

3. See the critique of this kind of theological positivism in D. Novak, *Jewish Social Ethics* (New York: Oxford University Press, 1992), 22–44.

4. For the distinction between *natural* and *revealed* theology, see Kant, *Critique of Pure Reason*, B659, who argues against the former and ignores the latter.

5. See Saadiah Gaon, *Book of Beliefs and Opinions*, 3.3, trans. S. Rosenblatt (New Haven, CT: Yale University Press, 1948), 145.

6. Saadiah Gaon, *The Book of Beliefs and Opinions*, 3. Pref., 137.

7. Saadiah Gaon, *The Book of Beliefs and Opinions*, 4.1, 181.

8. Saadiah Gaon, *The Book of Beliefs and Opinions*, 3, 138.

9. Saadiah Gaon, *The Book of Beliefs and Opinions*, 3.1, 139.

10. B. Yoma 67b re Lev. 18:4.

11. See H. A. Wolfson, *Philo* (Cambridge, MA: Harvard University Press, 1947), 1:188–89; 2:173–74. Cf. MT: Mamrim, 1.1 re Deut. 17:10.

12. This Jewish version of *agraphos nomos* is not what the rabbis called "Oral Torah" (*torah she-b'al peh*), which are revealed traditions transmitted verbally and not argued for rationally. See B. Gittin 60b re Hos. 8:12.

13. Saadiah Gaon, *The Book of Beliefs and Opinions*, 1.6.

14. They are called *al-samiah* in Arabic and *shim'iyot* in Hebrew. See Saadiah Gaon, *The Book of Beliefs and Opinions*, 3.3, 145.

15. See B. Berakhot 34b re Isa. 64:3.

16. See Kant, *Critique of Pure Reason*, B655–57.

17. See Alexandre Koyré, *From Closed World to the Infinite Universe* (Baltimore, MD: Johns Hopkins University Press, 1957). A. O. Lovejoy, *The Great Chain of Being* (Cambridge, MA: Harvard University Press, 1936).

18. See Maimonides, *Guide of the Perplexed*, 1.71, trans. S. Pines (Chicago: University of Chicago Press, 1963), 180.

19. Thus God is to be thanked as the ultimate giver of all benefits by those who have received them, yet this is because they have been commanded to thank God for these gifts. Their thanksgiving, then, is not spontaneous. See B. Berakhot 54b; *Beresheet Rabbah* 43.7 re Gen. 14:19; MT: Berakhot, 1.2–3.

20. See MT: Mattnot Aniyyim, 10.9.

21. M. Avot 6.2–3 re Num. 21:19 and Prov. 4:2; B. Shabbat 88a–b re Est. 9:27 and Prov. 11:3.

22. See Plato, *Republic*, 352C.

23. Scripture refers to this as "a man doing what is right [*yashar*] in his own eyes" (Judges 21:25). This is essentially different from the type of dispensations from legal statutes in particular circumstances which those who have public authority are entitled to make, that is, if ruling according to a specific statute would result in great injustice. See B. Baba Metsia 83a re Prov. 2:20. Cf. Plato, *Politicus*, 294A–295E; Aristotle, *Nicomachean Ethics*, 5.10/1137b20–25.

24. See for example LXX on Deut. 4:44.

25. This was most famously enunciated by David Hume, *A Treatise of Human Nature*, 3.1.1.

26. On this point, see my critique of John Finnis's *Natural Law and Natural Rights* (Oxford: Clarendon Press, 1980), 51–52 in D. Novak, *Athens and Jerusalem: God, Humans, and Nature* (Toronto: University of Toronto Press, 2019), 317, n. 64.

27. Abraham Joshua Heschel, *Who is Man?* (Stanford, CA: Stanford University Press, 1965), 97. On that same page, Heschel reminds us, "What Adam hears first is a command." He is referring to Gen. 2:16, "The Lord God commanded the human person [*ha'adam*]." Deferring to current sensibilities, I have avoided Heschel's use of "man" to denote the human species since in ordinary English "man" usually denotes the male gender. That *ha'adam* refers to all humans (like *anthrōpos* as distinct from *anēr* in Greek, or *Mensch* as distinct from *Mann* in German), regardless of gender, religion or ethnicity, see B. Sanhedrin 57b re Gen. 9:6 and 59a re Lev. 18:5 and *Tos.*, s.v. "ela"; B. Yevamot 61a and *Tos.*, s.v. "v'ein."

28. See for example M. Ketubot 9.2.

29. B. Sanhedrin 56b.

30. Gen. 1:25–30, 3:23; Ps. 115:16.

31. Gen. 4:10–11; Deut. 19:10, 21:7–9, 32:43; Joel 4:19; Job. 16:18; M. Sanhedrin 6.5

32. See MT: Rotseah, 4.9 re Prov. 28:17.

33. For the rabbinic version of the principle *nulla poena sine lege* see B. Sanhedrin 54a re Lev. 18:7.

34. Louis Ginzberg, *Legends of the Jews* (Philadelphia, PA: Jewish Publication Society of America, 1909–1938), 1:109; 5:139, n. 19.

35. For a similar claim to justice by a victim of injustice, see II Sam. 13:12–14; II Chron. 24:22.

36. B. Sanhedrin 73a re Lev. 19:16 and Deut. 22:26; ibid. 82a.

37. M. Ketubot 9.2. Cf. B. Baba Metsia 85a re Ps. 145:9.

38. The demand for vengeance is the reasonable demand that the harm you did to me be done to you accordingly and proportionally. As a victim, I have a right, that is, a justifiable claim that you (viz., all others) do not get away with what you have done to me wrongly. However, this is to be done by an impartial third party—the court—to avenge the crime committed against me reasonably (MT: Melakhim, 9.12). Concerning proportional justice, see B. Baba Kama 83b-84a re Lev. 24:17–22; M. Makkot 1.6 and B. Baba Kama 5a re Deut. 19:19–21; MT: Edut, 20.2; B. Makkot 12a re Num. 35:24; MT: Rotseah, 1.5.

39. On this point I respectfully disagree with the Jewish philosopher Emmanuel Levinas who, in his essay "The Rights of Man and the Rights of the Other" in

Outside the Subject, trans. M. B. Smith (Stanford, CA: Stanford University Press, 1994), writes, "These rights are in a sense *a priori* . . . prior to all entitlement. . . . These rights of man . . . do not need to be conferred, are thus irrevocable and inalienable" (116–17). However, a right can only be properly exercised when the rightholder knows he or she has been so entitled originally by God, who is the original right-holder, the only autonomous One, who entitles all subsequent rights-holders archetypally. *Pace* Levinas, a person's presence or "face" (*le visage*), which is their "otherness" (*l'autrement*), does not have this normative authority ipso facto. For a critique of Levinas, see Novak, *Athens and Jerusalem*, 238–43.

40. B. Sanhedrin 37b.

41. Cf. B. Kiddushin 19b and 32a–b for rights that may be waived.

42. B. Baba Kama 91b re Gen. 9:5. On the other hand, when faced with the choice of martyrdom (i.e., accept another religion or be killed), a Jew is obligated to die instead of exercising his or her right to life (B. Sanhedrin 74a–b; MT: Yesodei ha-Torah, 5.1–3). Nevertheless, anybody who didn't fulfill this onerous duty is judged to have acted under excusable duress *post factum* (MT: Yesodei ha-Torah, 5.4; see B. Baba Kama 28b re Deut. 22:26).

43. B. Sanhedrin 73a re Lev. 19:16.

44. See Ps. 31:6; Job 1:21; Eccl. 12:4; B. Niddah 31a.

45. It is pointed out in *Mekhilta*: Yitro 8, ed. Horovitz-Rabin, 233, that in the Decalogue, the five commandments on the first tablet (which pertain to the God-human relationship) parallel the five commandments on the second tablet (which pertain to interhuman relationships). Thus "I am the Lord your God" (Exod. 20:2) is parallel to "You shall not murder" (20:13). When one denies God, one therefore permits oneself to violate another human being; and when one violates another human being, one is ultimately intending to violate God. See also T. Yevamot 8.7 and *Beresheet Rabbah* 34.4 re Gen. 9:6.

46. As such, even those who positively contribute to human flourishing in the world are to be positively acknowledged. See B. Shabbat 33b (the opinion of Rabbi Judah regarding even the Roman rulers of Palestine); also M. Avot 3.2; B. Avodah Zarah 4a. Conversely, purposeless human destructiveness is condemned (B. Shabbat 105b re Ps. 81:10; comment of Isaac Abravanel on Deut. 20:19, citing II Kings 3:19).

47. Y. Nedarim 9.4/41c re Lev. 19:18 and Gen. 5:1.

48. M. Avot 3.14 re Gen. 9:6.

49. See Aristotle, *Nicomachean Ethics*, 5.5/1134a30.

50. See Novak, *Natural Law in Judaism*, 139–42.

51. LXX translates this verse "justly [*dikaiōs*] you shall pursue what is just [*to dikaion*]"; so too *Targum Jonathan ben Uziel*, viz. "a just ruling [*din qeshot*] justly [*bi-qeshot*].

52. See for example B. Baba Kama 113a–b; also, B. Yevamot 79a.

53. Josh. 1:1–4, 11:19; M. Yadayim 4.4 re Isa. 10:13; B. Sanhedrin 41a. Cf. Maimonides, *Sefer ha-Mitsvot*, pos. no. 187.

54. The first commandment commanded the first humans is for humans as political beings to establish courts of law to administer fair judgment (*dinin*) in both civil and

criminal matters (B. Sanhedrin 56a–b re Gen. 2:16; MT: Melakhims, 9.14; Saadiah Gaon, *The Book of Beliefs and Opinions*, 3.9 re Gen. 9:6).

55. Y. Sheviit 6.1/36c.

56. MT: Kings, 6.1–5 re Deut. 20:16 and 25:19.

57. MT: Kings, 8.10–9.1.

58. B. Sanhedrin 19a re Zeph. 2:1; B. Baba Metsia 59b.

59. B. Sanhedrin 59a. Cf. Cicero, *De Officiis*, 3.17.69.

60. B. Hagigah 3b re Eccl. 12:11.

61. B. Shabbat 23a, B. Berakhot 19b, and MT: Mamrim, 1.1 re Deut. 17:10–11.

62. In fact, God is to be appealed to for justice in this regard only when a one's human court is unable or unwilling to do so (See B. Baba Kama 93a).

63. B. Kiddushin 29a re Num. 15:23. Cf. T. Berakhot 1.12 re Jer. 23:7–8.

64. MT: Mamrim, 2.5–7.

65. Gen. 8:22; Jer. 33:19, 25.

66. MT: Melakhim, 8.11.

67. B. Kiddushin 31a, and the comment in the gloss in *Tos.*, s.v. "gadol."

68. B. Sanhedrin 6b re II Chron. 19:6.

69. B. Shabbat 10a re Exod. 18:13 and Gen. 1:5.

70. See B. Hagigah 12a re Gen. 1:1 and Isa. 66:1. Cosmic justice (what the Greeks called *dikē*) is akin to what Aristotle called "distributive justice" (*Nicomachean Ethics*, 5.3/1131a10–30), namely, an "allotment" (*dianomē*) appropriate to each being to which it has been distributed. It is not akin to what Aristotle called "rectifying justice" (*Nicomachean Ethics*, 5.4/131b25–1132a25), namely, a "correction" (*diorthōma*) since the nonhuman cosmos or nature hasn't the freedom to do injustice, hence there is nothing there to be corrected. Justice in the human world, though, is both allotment and judgment. Allotment is the entitlement of appropriate rights as just claims and the prescription of duties as the just responses to them. This kind of judgment (*mishpat*) is the rectification of the deeds of those who have freely violated the rights of others and who have thereby freely repudiated their duty. For judgment as rectification, see B. Sanhedrin 6b re Zech. 8:16. For justice as allotment, see for example B. Baba Batra 119b re Num. 27:7; also, B. Baba Kama 80b–81b.

71. *Shir ha-Shirim Rabbah*: Canticles 1.14 re Exod. 19:9.

Bibliography

ABBREVIATIONS

B. = *Babylonian Talmud (Bavli)*
LXX = Septuagint
M. = *Mishnah*
MT = Maimonides, *Mishneh Torah*
T. = *Tosefta*
Tos. = *Tosafot* (glosses on *Bavli*)
Y. = *Palestinian Talmud (Yerushalmi)*

CLASSICAL JUDAIC TEXTS

Abraham ben David of Posquières. Notes on *Mishneh Torah.*
Abraham ibn Ezra. *Commentary on the Torah*, 3 vols., ed. A. Weiser. Jerusalem: Mosad ha-Rav Kook, 1977.
————. *Commentary on Prophets and Writings* in *Miqraot Gedolot.*
Abravanel, Isaac. *Commentary on the Former Prophets.* Jerusalem: Torah ve-Daat, 1956.
Babylonian Talmud (Bavli), with comments of Rabbenu Hananel, Rashi and *Tosafot*, 20 vols. Vilna: Romm, 1898.
Bemidbar Rabbah in *Midrash Rabbah.*
Beresheet Rabbah, 4 vols., ed. J. Theodor and C. Albeck. Berlin: Akademie Verlag, 1912–1929.
Biblia Hebraica, 7th ed., ed. R. Kittel. Stuttgart: Priviligierte Württembergische Bibelanstalt, 1951.
Das Buch Yecheskel, trans. M. Buber. Berlin: Schocken Verlag.
Das Buch Yeschayahu, trans. M. Buber. Berlin: Schocken Verlag.
David Kimhi (Radak). *Commentary on the Latter Prophets in Miqraot Gedolot: Prophets and Writings.*
Devarim Rabbah in *Midrash Rabbah.*

Devarim Rabbah, ed. S. Lieberman. Jerusalem: Wahrmann Books, 1974.

Ecclesiasticus (Sirachides) in *Septuaginta*.

Esther Rabbah, ed. J. Tabory and A. Atzmon. Jerusalem: Schechter Institute, 2014.

Die Fünf Bücher der Weisung, trans. M. Buber and F. Rosenzweig. Cologne: Jakob Hegner, 1954.

Gikitala, Joseph. *Shaarei Orah*, 2 vols., ed. Y. Ben-Shlomo. Jerusalem: Mosad Bialik, 1981.

Ginzberg, Louis. *Legends of the Jews*, 7 vols. Philadelphia: Jewish Publication Society of America, 1909–1938.

Hayyim ibn Atar. *Commentary on the Torah* in *Miqraot Gedeolot*: Pentateuch.

Hezekiah ben Manoah (Hizquni). *Commentary on the Torah*, ed. C. B. Chavel. Jerusalem: Moasad ha-Rav Kook, 1982.

Holy Scriptures According to the Masoretic Text. Philadelphia: Jewish Publication Society, 1917.

Isaac Alfasi. *Hilkhot ha-Rif* with comments of Jonah Gerondi in *Babylonian Talmud*, ed. Vilna.

Isaac bar Sheshet Parfat. *Teshuvot ha-Rivash*. Jerusalem: Makhon Or ha-Mizrah, 1992.

Isaiah ha-Levi Horovitz. *Shnei Luhot ha-Berit*, 2 vols. Jerusalem, 1963.

Josephus. *Jewish Antiquities*, 6 vols., ed. and trans. H. St. John Thackeray, R. Marcus, A. Wikgren, and L. H. Feldman. Cambridge, MA: Harvard University Press, 1930–1965.

Judah Halevi. *Kitab al-khazari*, ed. H. Hirschfeld. London: Calingold, 1931.

———. *Kuzari*, trans. J. ibn Tibbon. Vilna: Romm, 1905.

———. *Sefer ha-Kuzari*, trans. Y. Even-Shmuel. Tel Aviv: Dvir, 1972.

———. *Kuzari: An Argument for the Faith of Israel*, trans. H. Hirschfeld. New York: Schocken, 1964.

———. *Selected Poems*, ed. H. Brody, trans. N. Salaman. Philadelphia: Jewish Publication Society of America, 1924.

Karo, Joseph. *Kesef Mishneh* in Maimonides, *Mishneh Torah*.

———. *Shulhan Arukh*, 7 vols. Lemberg, 1873.

The Koren Mahzor: Yamim Noraim. Jerusalem: Koren, 2018.

Maimonides. *Commentary on the Mishnah*, 3 vols., ed. and trans. Y. Kafih. Jerusalem: Mosad ha-Rav Kook, 1964–1967.

———. *Dalalat al-ha'irin*, ed. S. Munk and I. Joel. Jerusalem: J. Junovitch, 1931.

———. *Guide of the Perplexed*, trans. S. Pines. Chicago: University of Chicago Press, 1963.

———. *Igrot ha-Rambam*, 2 vols., ed. and trans. I. Shailat. Maaleh Adumim: Maaliyot Press, 1988.

———. *Mishneh Torah*, 12 vols., ed. S. Frankel. Bnai Brak: Shabse Frankel, 2001.

———. *Moreh Nevukhim*, trans. S. ibn Tibbon. New York: Om, 1946.

———. *Sefer ha-Mitsvot*, ed. C. Heller. Jerusalem: Mosad ha-Rav Kook, 1946.

———. *Teshuvot ha-Rambam*, 3 vols., ed. Y. Blau. Jerusalem: Meqitsei Nirdamim, 1960.

Meir ibn Gabbai. *Avodat ha-Qodesh*. Jerusalem: Lewin-Epstein, 1954.

Mekhilta de-Rabbi Ishmael, ed. S. H. Horovitz and I. A. Rabin. Jerusalem: Wahrmann, 1960.

Menahem ha- Meiri. *Bet ha-Behirah*: B. Berakhot, ed. S. Dikman. Jerusalem: Makhon ha-Talmud ha-Yisraeli ha-Shalem, 1960.

———. *Bet ha-Behirah*: B. Avodah Zarah, ed. A. Sofer. Jerusalem: Kedem, 1961.

Midrash ha-Gadol: Beresheet, ed. M. Margulies. Jerusalem: Mosad ha-Rav Kook, 1966.

Midrash Rabbah. 2 vols. New York: Anafim, 1957.

Midrash Tehillim, ed. S. Buber. Vilna: Romm, 1891.

Miqraot Gedolot: Pentateuch, 5 vols. New York: Otsar ha-Sefarim, 1953.

Miqraot Gedolot: Prophets and Writings, 3 vols. New York: Pardes, 1951.

Mishnah, 12 vols, with comments by Obadiah Bertinoro, Yom Tov Lipmann Heller, and Israel Lifshitz. New York: M. P. Press, 1969.

Mishnah, 6 vols., ed. C. Albeck. Tel Aviv: Mosad Bialik and Dvir, 1957.

Mishnat Rabbi Eliezer, 2 vols., ed. H. G. Enelow. New York: Bloch Publishing, 1933.

Mishnat ha-Zohar, 2 vols., ed. Y. Tishbi. Jerusalem: Mosad Bialik, 1957.

Nahmanides (Ramban). *Commentary on the Torah,* 2 vols. ed. C. B. Chavel. Jerusalem: Mosad ha-Rav Kook, 1959–1963.

———. *Hiddushei ha-Ramban,* 2 vols. Bnei Brak: 1959.

———. *Kitvei Ramban,* 2 vols., ed. C. B. Chavel. Jerusalem: Mosad ha-Rav Kook, 1963.

Obadiah Bertinoro. *Commentary on the Mishnah* in *Mishnayot,* 12 vols. New York, 1969.

Obadiah Sforno. *Commentary on the Torah,* ed. Z. Gottlieb. Jerusalem: Mosad ha-Rav Kook, 1980.

Otsar ha-Geonim: Berakhot, ed. B. M. Lewin. Haifa, 1928.

Otsar ha-Geonim: Hagigah, ed. B. M. Lewin. Jerusalem: Hebrew University, 1931.

Palestinian Talmud (Yerushalmi), ed. Pietrkov, with D. Franekel, *Qorban ha`Edah* and M. Margolis, *Pnei* Mosheh, 7 vols. Jerusalem, 1959.

———. ed. Y. Sussmann. Jerusalem: Academy of the Hebrew Language, 2001.

Pesiqta Rabbati, ed. M. Friedmann. Vienna, 1880.

Pesiqta de-Rav Kahana, 2 vols., ed. B. Mandelbaum. New York: Jewish Theological Seminary of America, 1962.

Philo, 10 vols., trans. F. H. Colson and G. H. Whitaker. Cambridge, MA: Harvard University Press, 1939–1962.

Rashi. *Commentary on the Torah,* ed. C. B. Chavel. Jerusalem: Mosad ha-Rav Kook, 1982.

———. *Commentary on the Talmud* in *Babylonian Talmud.*

Saadiah Gaon. *The Book of Beliefs and Opinions,* trans. S. Rosenblatt. New Haven, CT: Yale University Press, 1948.

———. *Commentary on the Torah,* ed. Y. Kafih Jerusalem: Mosad ha-Rav Kook, 1963.

———. *Kitab al-amanat wal-Itikadat,* ed. and trans. J. Kafih. Jerusalem, 1960.

Septuaginta, 6th ed., 2 vols., ed. A. Rahlfs. Stuttgart: Privilegierte Württembergische Bibelanstalt, 1952.

Shemot Rabbah in *Midrash Rabbah*.
————. ed. A. Shinan. Jerusalem: Dvir, 1984.
Shir ha-Shirim Rabbah in *Midrash Rabbah*.
Sifra, ed. I. H. Weiss. New York: Om, 1947.
Sifre: Devarim, ed. Louis Finkelstein. New York: Jewish Theological Seminary of America, 1969.
Shemot Rabbah in *Midrash Rabbah*.
————. ed. A. Shinan. Jerusalem: Dvir, 1984.
Sofrim, ed. M. Higger. Jerusalem: Makor, 1969.
Tanhuma, Jerusalem: Lewin-Epstein, 1962.
Targum Jonathan ben Uziel in *Miqraot Gedolot*: Pentateuch.
Targum Onqelos in *Miqraot Gedolot*: Prophets and Writings.
The Torah, 2nd ed. Philadelphia, PA.: Jewish Publication Society of America, 1962.
Tosafot in Babylonian Talmud.
Tosefta, 5 vols., ed. S. Lieberman. New York: Jewish Theological Seminary of America, 1955–1988.
Tosefta, ed. S. Zuckermandl. Jerusalem: Wahrmann Books, 1937.
Tosefta, 5 vols., ed. S. Lieberman. New York: Jewish Theological Seminary of America, 1955–1988.
The Traditional Prayer Book for Sabbath and Festivals, trans. D. de Sola Pool. New York: Behrman House, 1960.
Vayiqra Rabbah, 4 vols., ed. M. Margulies. Jerusalem: American Academy for Jewish Research, 1953–1956.
Wisdom of Solomon in *Septuaginta*.
Yair Hayyim Bachrach. *Responsa: Havot Yair*. Jerusalem.
Yalqut Shimoni, 2 vols. New York: Title Publishing, 1944.
Zohar, 3 vols., ed. R. Margaliot. Jerusalem: Mosad ha-Rav Kook, 1970.
Zohar, 12 vols., trans. and annotated D. Matt. Stanford, CA: Stanford University Press, 2004–2018.

CLASSICAL TEXTS

Anselm. *Proslogion* in *St. Anselm: Basic Writings*, trans. S. N. Deane. LaSalle, IL: Open Court, 1962.
Aristotle. *Metaphysics*, 2 vols., ed. and trans. H. Tredennick. Cambridge, MA: Harvard University Press, 1933.
————. *Nicomachean Ethics*. ed. and trans. H. Rackham. Cambridge, MA: Harvard University Press, 1926.
————. *Politics*, ed. and trans. H. Rackham. Cambridge, MA: Harvard University Press, 1932.
————. *Posterior Analytics*, ed. and trans. H. Tredennick. Cambridge, MA: Harvard University Press, 1960.
Cicero. *De Officiis*, trans. J. Higginbotham. London: Faber & Faber, 1967.

John of Damascus. "On the Orthodox Faith," *Saint John of Damascus: Writings*, trans. F. H. Chase Jr. New York: Fathers of the Church, 1958.

Novum Testamentum Graece, 24th ed., ed. E. Nestle. Stuttgart: Privilegierte Württembergische Bibelanstalt, 1960.

Origen. *Origenes Hexaplorum*, ed. F. Field. Oxford: Clarendon Press, 1873.

Plato. *Apology*, ed. and trans. H. N. Fowler. Cambridge, MA: Harvard University Press, 1914.

―――. *Phaedrus*, ed. and trans. H. N. Fowler. Cambridge, MA: Harvard University Press, 1914.

―――. *Politicus*, ed. and trans. H. N. Fowler. Cambridge, MA: Harvard University Press, 1925.

―――. *Republic*, 2 vols., ed. and trans. P. Shorey. Cambridge, MA: Harvard University Press, 1953.

Plotinus. *Enneads*, 7 vols., ed. and trans. A. H. Armstrong. Cambridge, MA: Harvard University Press, 1966–1988.

Quran, trans. H. M. N. Ahmad. London: The London Mosque, 1981.

Thomas Aquinas. *Lectura romana in primum Sentiarum Petri Lombardi*, ed. and annotated L. E. Boyle and J. F. Boyle. Toronto: Pontifical Institute of Mediaeval Studies, 2006.

―――. *Quaestiones disputatae de veritate*, ed. E. Stein. Breslau: Borgmeyer, 1931.

―――. *Summa Contra Gentiles*, 5 vols., trans. A. C. Pegis. Garden City, NY: Image Books, 1955–1956.

―――. *Summa Theologiae*, 3 vols., ed. P. Caramello. Rome: Marietti, 1962.

―――. *Summa Theologiae*, 2 vols., in *Basic Writings of Saint Thomas Aquinas*, ed. A. Pegis. New York: Random House, 1945.

Vulgate, 3 vols. Paris: Garnier, 1922.

MODERN JUDAIC TEXTS

Altmann, Alexander. "What Is Jewish Theology?" in *The Meaning of Jewish Existence: Theological Essays*, trans. E. Ehrlich and L. H. Ehrlich, ed. A. Ivry. Hanover, NH: University Press of New England, 1991.

Buber, Martin. *Between Man and Man*, trans. R. G. Smith. Boston: Beacon Press, 1955.

―――. *I and Thou*, trans. Walter Kaufmann. New York: Scribner's, 1970.

―――. *Ich und Du*. Heidelberg: Verlag Lambert Schneider, 1962.

―――. *The Kingship of God*, 3rd rev. ed., trans. R. Scheimann. New York: Harper & Row, 1967.

―――. *Zu einer neuen Verdeutschung der Schrift*. Olten: Jakob Hegner, 1954.

Cassuto, Umberto. *A Commentary on the Book of Exodus*, trans. I. Abrahams. Jerusalem: Magnes Press, 1967.

Cohen, Hermann. *Begriff der Religion im System der Philosophie*. Giessen: A. Töpelmann, 1915.

———. *Religion der Vernunft aus den Quellen des Judentums*, 2nd ed. Darmstadt: Joseph Melzer Verlag, 1966.

———. *Religion of Reason Out of the Sources of Judaism*, trans. S. Kaplan. New York: Frederick Ungar, 1972.

Eleh Divrei ha-Berit, ed. Moses Schreiber. Altona, n.p., 1819.

Fackenheim, Emil. *God's Presence in History*. New York: New York University Press, 1970.

Galli, Barbara E. *Franz Rosenzweig and Jehuda Halevi*. Montreal: McGill-Queens University Press, 1995.

Geiger, Abraham. *Nachgelassene Schriften*, 2 vols., ed. L. Geiger. Berlin: Louis Gerschel, 1875.

Halivni, David Weiss. *Revelation Restored*. New York: Routledge, 2018.

Heinemann, Yizhak. *The Reasons for the Commandments in Jewish Thought*, trans. L. Levin. Boston: Academic Studies Press, 2008.

Heschel, Abraham Joshua. *God in Search of Man*. New York: Farrar, Straus & Cudahy, 1955.

———. *Heavenly Torah*, trans. G. Tucker and L. Levin. New York: Continuum, 2005.

———. *Man Is Not Alone*. Philadelphia: Jewish Publication Society of America, 1951.

———. *Die Prophetie*. Warsaw: Polish Academy of Sciences, 1936.

———. *The Prophets*. Philadelphia: Jewish Publication Society of America, 1962.

———. *Who Is Man?* Stanford, CA: Stanford University Press, 1965.

Jacobson, E. "The Future of Kabbalah" in *Kabbalah and Modernity*, ed. B. Huss, M. Pasi, and K. von Struckand. Leiden: Brill, 2010.

Kasher, M. M. *Torah Shelemah*, 11 vols., Jerusalem: Torah Shelemah Institute, 1992.

Katz, Jacob. *Halakhah ve-Kabbalah*. Jerusalem: Magnes Press, 1986.

Kellner, Menachem. *Dogma in Mediaeval Jewish Thought*. Oxford: Oxford University Press, 1986.

Kohut, Alexander. *Arukh ha-Shalem*, 9 vols. Tel Aviv: Shilo, 1970.

Krauss, Samuel. "Trinity," *Jewish Encyclopedia* 12 (1905): 260–61.

Lieberman, Saul. *Hellenism in Jewish Palestine*, 2nd ed., New York: Jewish Theological Seminary of America, 1962.

———. *Tosefta Ki-fshuta*, 11 vols. New York: Jewish Theological Seminary of America, 1955–1988.

Marmorstein, A. *The Old Rabbinic Doctrine of God*. London: Oxford University Press, 1927.

Mendelssohn, Moses. *Jerusalem*, trans. A. Arkush. Hanover, NH: University Press of New England, 1983.

Meyers, Carol. *Exodus*. Cambridge: Cambridge University Press, 2005.

Novak, David. *Athens and Jerusalem*. Toronto: University of Toronto Press, 2019.

———. "Buber's Critique of Heidegger," *Modern Judaism* 5 (1985): 125–40.

———. *Covenantal Rights*. Princeton, NJ: Princeton University Press, 2000.

———. "Creation" in *The Cambridge History of Jewish Philosophy: The Modern Era*, ed. M. Kavka, Z. Braiterman and D. Novak. Cambridge: Cambridge University Press, 2012.

————. "Heschel's Phenomenology of Revelation" in *Abraham Joshua Heschel: Philosophy, Theology and Interreligious Dialogue*, ed. S Krajewski and A. Lypszyc. Wiesbaden: Harrowitz Verlag, 2009.

————. *The Image of the Non-Jew in Judaism*, 2nd ed., ed. M. LaGrone. Oxford: Littman Library, 2011.

————. *Jewish Justice*. Waco, TX: Baylor University Press, 2017.

————. *Jewish Social Ethics*. New York: Oxford University Press, 1992.

————. *Law and Theology in Judaism*, 2 vols. New York: KTAV, 1974–1976.

————. *Natural law in Judaism*. Cambridge: Cambridge University Press, 1998.

————. *Natural Law: A Jewish, Christian, and Islamic Trialogue* with Anver Emon and Matthew Levering. Oxford: Oxford University Press, 2014.

————. "The Self-Contraction of the Godhead in Kabbalistic Theology" in *Neoplatonism and Jewish Thought*, ed. L. E. Goodman. Albany: SUNY Press, 1992.

————. "The Talmud as a Source for Philosophical Reflection," in *History of Jewish Philosophy*, ed. D. H. Frank and O. Leaman. New York: Routledge, 1997.

————. *The Theology of Nahmanides Systematically Presented*. Atlanta, GA: Scholars Press, 1992.

————. *Zionism and Judaism: A New Theory*. Cambridge: Cambridge University Press, 2015.

Prayers for the Day of Atonement, trans. D. de Sola Pool. New York: Union of Sephardic Congregations, 1967.

Rosenzweig, Franz. *Jehudah Halevi: Zweiunneunzig Hymnen und Gedichte*. Verlag Lambert Schneider.

————. *Kleinere Schriften*, ed. Edith Rosenzweig. Berlin: Schocken Verlag, 1937.

————. *On Jewish Learning*, trans. N. N. Glatzer and W. Wolf. New York: Schocken, 1955.

————. *Philosophical and Theological Writings*, trans. P. W. Franks and M. L. Morgan. Bloomington: Indiana University Press, 2000.

————. *The Star of Redemption*, trans. B. E. Galli. Madison: University of Wisconsin Press, 2005.

————. *Der Stern der Erlösung*. Frankfurt am-Main: Kaufmann Verlag, 1921.

Scholem, Gershom. *Major Trends in Jewish Mysticism*, 3rd rev. ed. New York: Schocken, 1954.

————. *On the Kabbalah and Its Symbolism*, trans. R. Manheim. New York: Schocken, 1969.

————. *Origins of Kabbalah*, trans. A. Arkush. Princeton, NJ: Princeton University Press, 1987.

————. "Schöpfung aus Nichts und die Selbstverschränkung Gottes," *Eranos Jahrbuch* 25 (1956): 87–119.

Schreiber, Moses. *Responsa: Hatam Sofer*, 3 vols. New York, 1958.

Stern, Gregg. *Philosophy and Rabbinic Culture*. London: Routledge, 2009.

Tishby, Y. *Mishnat ha-Zohar*, 2nd ed. 2 vols. Jerusalem: Mosad Bialik, 1957.

Wolfson, Elliot R. *Through a Speculum That Shines*. Princeton, NJ: Princeton University Press, 1994.

Wolfson, H. A. *Philo*, 2 vols. Cambridge, MA: Harvard University Press, 1947.

————. *The Philosophy of Spinoza*, 2 vols., Cambridge, MA: Harvard University Press, 1934.

MODERN TEXTS (GENERAL)

Anscombe, G. E. M. *Intention*, 2nd ed. Ithaca, NY: Cornell University Press, 1963.

Auden, W. H. "September 1, 1939" in *Seven Centuries of Verse: English and American*, ed. A. J. M. Smith. New York: Scribner's, 1957.

Ayer, A. J. *Language, Truth, and Logic*. New York: Dover Publications, 1952.

Barth, Karl. *Church Dogmatics*, 2/1, trans. G. T. Thomson and N. Knight. Edinburgh: T. & T. Clark, 2009.

————. *Fides Quaerens Intellectum*, trans. I. W. Robertson. London: SCM Press, 1960.

————. *Kirchliche Dogmatik*, 2/1. Frankfurt am-Main: Fischer Bücherei, 1955.

Buber, Martin. *Between Man and Man*, trans. R. G. Smith. Boston: Beacon Press, 1955.

————. *I and Thou*, trans. W. Kaufmann. New York: Chas. Scribner's Sons, 1970.

————. *Ich und Du*. Heidelberg: Verlag Lambert Schneider, 1962.

————. *Werkausgabe*, 21 vols. Gütersloh: Gütersloh Verlaghaus, 2002–2020.

Cherbonnier, E. LaB. "The Logic of Biblical Anthropomorphism," *Harvard Theological Review* 55 (1962): 187–206.

Cohen, Hermann. *Ethik des reinen Willens*, 5th ed. Hildesheim: Georg Olms Verlag, 1981.

————. *Logik der reinen Erkenntnis*, 4th ed. Hildesheim: Georg Olms Verlag, 1977.

Cover, Robert. "Nomos and Narrative," *Narrative, Violence, and Law*, ed. M. Minow et al. Ann Arbor: University of Michigan Press, 1992.

Durkheim. Émile, *Elementary Forms of the Religious Life*, trans. J. W. Swain. New York: Free Press, 1965.

Eliot, T. S. *The Idea of a Christian Society*, 2nd ed. London: Faber & Faber, 1982.

————. "Murder in the Cathedral," *Complete Poems and Plays: 1909–1950*. New York: Harcourt, Brace & World, 1971.

Finnis, John. *Natural Law and Natural Rights*. Oxford: Clarendon Press, 1980.

Fraade, Steven D. "Nomos and Narrative," *Yale Journal of Law and Humanities* 17 (2005): 81–96.

Freud, Sigmund. *The Future of an Illusion*, trans. W. D. Robson-Scott, rev. J. Strachey. Garden City, NY: Anchor Books, 1964.

Gadamer, Hans-Georg. *Truth and Method*. New York: Crossroad, 1982.

Gilson, Étienne. *God and Philosophy*, 2nd ed. New Haven, CT: Yale University Press, 2002.

————. *The Spirit of Mediaeval Philosophy*, trans. A. H. C. Downes. London: Sheed and Ward, 1936.

Goodman, Lenn E. *Avicenna*. New York: Routledge, 1992.

Hartshorne, Charles, and W. L. Reese. *Philosophers Speak of God*. Chicago: University of Chicago Press, 1987.

Heidegger, Martin. *Being and Time*, trans. J. Stambaugh. Albany: SUNY Press, 1996.

————. *Sein und Zeit*, 15th ed., Tübingen: Max Niemeyer Verlag, 1979.

————. "Vom Wesen der Wahrheit," *Wegmarken*, 4th ed. Frankfurt am-Main: Vittorio Klostermann Verlag, 1967.

Hume, David. *Dialogues Concerning Natural Religion*, ed. H. D. Aiken. New York: Hafner, 1959.

————. *A Treatise of Human Nature*, ed. L. A. Selby-Bigge. Oxford: Clarendon Press, 1888.

Isaacson, Walter. *Leonardo da Vinci*. New York: Simon & Schuster, 2017.

Kant, Immanuel. *Critique of Practical Reason*, trans. W. S. Pluhar. Indianapolis, IN: Hackett Publishing, 2002.

————. *Critique of Pure Reason*, trans. N. Kemp Smith. New York: Macmillan, 1929.

————. *Kritik der reinen Vernunft*, ed. R. Schmidt. Hamburg: Felix Meiner Verlag, 1956.

Kautzsch, Emil. *Die Heilige Schrift des Alten Testament*. Freiburg: J. C. B. Mohr/P. Siebeck, 1896.

Koyré, Alexandre. *From the Closed World to the Infinite Universe*. Baltimore, MD: Johns Hopkins University Press, 1957.

Levering, Matthew. *Scripture and Metaphysics*. Oxford: Blackwell, 2004.

Levinas, Emmanuel. *Outside the Subject*, trans. M. B. Smith. Stanford, CA: Stanford University Press, 1994.

————. *Totality and Infinity*, trans. A. Lingis. Pittsburgh, PA: Duquesne University Press, 1969.

Lovejoy, A. O. *The Great Chain of Being*. Cambridge, MA: Harvard University Press, 1936.

Mac Cumhall, C., and R. Wiseman. *Metaphysical Animals*. New York: Doubleday, 2022.

Marion, Jean-Luc. *God Without Being*, trans. T. A. Carlson. Chicago: University of Chicago Press, 1991.

Maritain, Jacques. *Existence and the Existent*, trans. L. Galantierre and G. B. Phelan. Garden City, NY: Image Books, 1956.

Niebuhr, Reinhold. *The Nature and Destiny of Man*, 2 vols. New York: Scribner's, 1943.

Nietzsche, Friedrich. *Also Sprach Zarathustra* in *Werke*, 2 vols., ed. K. Schlechta. Munich: Carl Hanser Verlag, 1967.

Novak, David. "On Freud's Theory of Law and Religion," *International Journal of Law and Psychiatry* 48 (2016): 24–34.

————. *Suicide and Morality*. New York: Scholars Studies Press, 1975.

Plantinga. Alvin, "Verificationism and Other Atheologica," *God and Other Minds*. Ithaca, NY: Cornell University Press, 1967.

Polanyi, Michael. *Personal Knowledge*. New York: Harper Torchbooks, 1962.

Riceour, Paul. "The Language of Faith," *The Philosophy of Paul Riceour*, ed. C. E. Reagan and D. Stewart. Boston: Beacon Press, 1998.

Rorty, Richard. "Religion as Conversation Stopper," *Common Knowledge* 3 (1994): 1–6.

Shah, Z. Ali. *Anthropomorphic Depictions of God*. London: International Institute of Islamic Thought, 2012.

Sokolowski, Robert. *Introduction to Phenomenology*. Cambridge: Cambridge University Press, 2000.

Soulen, R. Kendall. *Irrevocable*. Minneapolis, MN: Fortress Press, 2022.

Spinoza, Baruch. *Ethics* in *Opera*, vol. 2, ed. C. Gebhardt. Heidelberg: Carl Winter, 1925.

———. *Ethics*, trans. E. Curley in *A Spinoza Reader*. Princeton, NJ: Princeton University Press, 1994.

Strauss, Leo. *Philosophy and Law*, trans. E. Adler. Albany: SUNY Press, 1995.

Torrance, T. F. *Divine and Contingent Order*. Oxford: Oxford University Press, 1981.

Weinandy, Thomas. *Does God Suffer?* Notre Dame, IN: University of Notre Dame Press, 2004.

Wittgenstein, Ludwig. *Philosophical Investigations*, 2nd ed., ed. and trans. G. E. M. Anscombe. New York: Macmillan, 1958.

———. *Tractatus Logico-Philosophicus*, trans. D. F. Pears and B. F. McGuiness. London: Routledge and Kegan Paul, 1961.

Index

About the Author

David Novak is the J. Richard and Dorothy Shiff Chair of Jewish Studies Emeritus at the University of Toronto, where he is currently a fellow of St. Michael's College. He is also a founder and president of the Union for Traditional Judaism and a founder and vice president of the Institute on Religion and Public Life. *God-Talk: The Heart of Judaism* is his twentieth book.